MW01486946

CHRIST,
MY
HEALER!

NICKY
RAIBORDE

FURROW
PRESS

Christ, My Healer!
Copyright © 2010 by Nicky Raiborde
Published by Furrow Press
P.O. Box 98
Big Flats, NY 14814-0098

All Scripture quotations, unless otherwise marked, are from The New King James
Version, copyright © 1979, 1980, 1982 by Thomas Nelson Inc., Publishers.
Used by permission.

References noted as AMP are from The Amplified Bible. The Amplified Bible,
Old Testament, copyright © 1965, 1987 by The Zondervan Corporation.
The Amplified New Testament, copyright © 1954, 1958, 1987 by The Lockman
Foundation. Used by permission.

References noted as KJV are taken from the King James Version of the Bible.

References noted as LB are from the Living Bible copyright © 1971 by Tyndale
House Publishers, Wheaton, Ill. Used by permission.

References noted as MSG are from The Message copyright © by Eugene H. Peterson,
1993, 1994, 1995, 1996. Used by permission of NavPress Publishing Group.

Edited by Edie Mourey (www.furrowpress.com).

Cover design by Peter Sam, Singapore.

Interior design by David G. Danglis / Pinwheel Creative.

All rights reserved. This book or parts thereof may not be reproduced in any form,
except for brief quotations in reviews, without written permission from the publisher.

Printed in the United States of America.
Library of Congress Control Number: 2001012345
International Standard Book Number: 978-0-9800196-4-3

Dedicated to
Lim Lip Yong

I thank God for putting you in my life.
Your friendship means the world to me.
Your encouragement and transparency have helped me
walk steadily on the paths God has for my life.
I really appreciate you!

Contents

CHAPTER 1

The Blessing of Healing

*"Beloved, I pray that you may prosper in all things
and be in health, just as your soul prospers."*

3 JOHN 1:2

I giggled when my friend, John, recently said, "I have a razor-sharp memory. It's just short!" This was his poor excuse for forgetting his wedding anniversary.

Memory is a frightening tattletale. It reveals our true and immediate priorities, identifying what's most important to us right now. In John's situation, his forgetfulness didn't mean his marriage and his wife weren't important to him. His forgetfulness simply showed that something else in the *now* had pushed them into the recesses of his mind.

The psalmist reminds himself and us in Psalm 103:2 to bless the Lord "and forget not all His benefits." In our walks with God, we would do well to always keep our memories razor-sharp when it comes to the things that God has done and is doing for us. We need to make sure we don't allow other things or even wrong priorities to crowd Him out. We especially don't want to forget the benefits that He has provided for us.

One of the many benefits that God has provided for us is healing. Healing belongs to us. Healing is ours by the stripes that Jesus received (Isaiah 53:5), and it's given to us freely. As James 1:17 declares, "Every good gift and every perfect gift is from above, and comes down from the Father of lights, with whom there is no variation or shadow of turning." Healing is one of the "perfect" gifts given to us by our Father. It's a blessing from Him!

Sickness—Our Enemy

I believe all Christians may recognize the blessing of healing and the anguish of sickness and disease. Their theology on healing and sickness, on the other hand, can differ greatly. For example, I've heard some Christians assert that *sickness is God's will.* I've heard others teach that *sickness is a gift from God*, humbling us and drawing us closer to Him. I've even heard some testify that *God's purpose in their sickness is to teach* them.

I don't mean to be offensive, but such reasoning seems absurd to me! If a man really believed sickness is God's will, then I would expect him to do *nothing* for himself to receive comfort, relief, or healing. I would expect him *not* to go to the doctor or *not* to take medicine. And we've all heard stories of a few who have taken such stances. But more often than not, most of us run to various remedies for relief when we're sick, even many of those who claim sickness is God's will.

And as far as those who view sickness as a gift from God, I have one question for them: Why is it we never hear people crying out for a sickness or a disease? Think about it. When have you ever heard someone at the altar pray, "Lord, please give me a tumor"? How crazy would that be?!

Furthermore, if a father had the ability to cause his child to become sick and actually did so, we would lock him up for child abuse. God isn't a perpetrator of child abuse. He's a life-giving Father who "daily loads us with benefits" (Psalm 68:19) and whose gifts to us are good and perfect (James 1:17).

And yes, God *may* teach us something while we're sick; after all, He's able to redeem every situation and circumstance, creatively using them to draw us closer to Him and to instruct us about Him and His ways. But making a doctrine out of His making me sick so that He can teach me something is going too far. Remember, *God also teaches us when we're healthy*. Just because a woman, for example, may be learning spiritual lessons while she's ill doesn't explain her sickness, nor does it mean that it's God's best for her. We must realize *sickness is our enemy*.

In 1 Corinthians 15:26, Paul writes, "The last enemy *that* will be destroyed *is* death." If Paul calls death the enemy, I would think those sicknesses and diseases that work death in our physical bodies should be seen as death's friends. And any friend of death—any friend of my enemy—*is* my enemy!

Even those who aren't Christians and don't believe in Jesus perceive sickness isn't for them; it's against them. They understand that sickness is bad and not good. How do we know this? Just look at secular advertising slogans that say things like, "Fight AIDS," "Fight Cancer," or "Fight Diabetes."

Looking back at our opening verse in 3 John 1:2, we see the beloved apostle John as he expresses the very heart of God for us to be in health. He writes, "Beloved, I pray that you may prosper in all things and be in health, just as your soul prospers." This is the Father's desire for us. After all, our bodies are the temple of the Holy Spirit (1 Corinthians 6:19). How could anyone believe that the One who wants us to prosper and be in health is the same One who puts sickness on what He calls His own temple? There are those who don't have this understanding, so they teach that God puts sickness on people. Such people read Scriptures that say God sent sickness, or God afflicted so-and-so with severe disease, and they make a doctrine out of these—that all sickness is sent by Him.

If Paul calls death the enemy, I would think those sicknesses and diseases that work death in our physical bodies should be seen as death's friends.

In Deuteronomy 28:58-59, Moses instructs the Israelites saying, "'If you do not carefully observe all the words of this law that are written in this book . . . the LORD will bring upon you and your descendants extraordinary plagues . . . and serious and prolonged sicknesses.'" When we read this Scripture that says God will put plagues and sickness upon them, it simply means that His law of sowing and reaping will be executed and enforced by the proper agencies.

God has established His laws, and we face the consequences for breaking them. So many times when Scripture says God afflicted people or sent sickness upon them, if we read the context of what's happening, we'll discover that the people broke certain laws of God and called the sickness, the disease, or those forms of evil upon themselves. Sins of all kinds—rebellion, hardness of heart, fleshly lusts, pride, unbelief, and many other personal acts on the part of people—have caused them to break the laws of God and given the agents of sin, sickness, and death the opportunity to wreak havoc in their lives.

So we see in Scripture and in life that some sickness is the *direct result* of sin in an individual's life. Sickness, however, may also be an *indirect result* of sin. We do know that since the fall of man—since Adam and Eve sinned in the Garden of Eden—humanity experiences sickness, disease, pain, and suffering. This means that sickness and disease happen to both the righteous and the unrighteous, to those who are in Christ and those who aren't. Humanity experiences the wages of sin—death working in the human body (Romans 6:23). But Jesus came to give us the gift of God—eternal life. In fact, He proclaimed, "'I have come that they may have life, and that they may have it more abundantly'" (John 10:10).

If you're in Christ, He's already defeated sin and death for you. He's personally come to you to give you the abundant life. And the abundant life means that all He purchased for you on the cross—redemption, restoration, salvation, wholeness, and healing—is yours.

Healing—God's Provision

Recently, a lady approached me asking if I could go and pray for her sister who was suffering with a prolonged sickness. Her situation was very severe. When I went to see the sister, I asked her permission to pray for her. She responded by saying, "This is the cross I have to carry. I've been prayed over many times, but nothing has happened, and I don't think this is meant to be healed." So much for her confession of faith!

You see, delay and hope deferred, maybe even wrong teaching and influence, had built a stronghold in her life. She had started twisting Scriptures to justify why she wasn't receiving her healing. I explained to her that the cross she was referring to from Luke 9:23 was a cross of self-denial. Jesus said in that verse, "'If *anyone* desires to come after Me, let him deny himself, and take up his cross daily, and follow Me'" (emphasis added). The words here are addressed to "anyone" who would be a follower of Jesus. Every believer is called to self-denial, but not to sickness. I encouraged the sister about God's willingness and ability to heal. And then I prayed for her with her faith freshly fanned by the truth of God's Word.

> Every believer is called to self-denial, but not to sickness.

God wants you and me to live lives that bring glory to Him, and sickness doesn't bring glory to Him. Can He receive glory for healing us from sickness and disease? Yes! Can we give Him glory in the midst of our sickness and pain? Yes! But our being sick, in and of itself, doesn't glorify Him.

I want you, dear reader, to realize how much God desires to see you well and whole. I've seen God perform wonderful healings, even what I call *miracle healings*. I remember one such healing when my father was ministering. A man was listening in the audience and was very skeptical of the power of God. Yet God wanted to demonstrate His love for him. This man had no right thumb, as it had been cut off in an accident. Suddenly, the Holy Spirit created a thumb. It literally grew in front of the man's eyes! Wow!

The Gospels are replete with similar stories of miraculous healings where Jesus even created missing body parts. Matthew records an event where Jesus healed people who were maimed. The text reads, "Then great multitudes came to Him, having with them *the* lame, blind, mute, maimed, and many others; and they laid them down at Jesus' feet, and He healed them" (Matthew 15:30). According to *Strong's Exhaustive Concordance of the Bible*, the Greek word for *maimed* in this verse is the word *kullos* ("Greek Dictionary of the New Testament," 44). It refers to a person who is missing body parts. I know other versions translate this word as cripple, but a cripple is someone who has a part that can't function. It's evident from Scripture and from my own experience that God can heal cripples, and such a healing is indeed incredible and miraculous. Creative miracles like Jesus did in Matthew 15 and like the one my father witnessed, though, are other worldly. They display a greater dimension of the awesomeness of our God!

Another passage in Matthew says, "The multitude marveled [were amazed], when they saw *the* mute speaking, *the* maimed made whole, *the* lame walking, and *the* blind seeing" (18:8). You see the Bible is very clear that Christ is able to bring healing to the worst cases of sickness and disease—to those who are lame, maimed, blind, and mute.

As you read this book, I really want you to realize that no matter how bad your condition is, nor how long you have had this condition, Jesus is still in the business of bringing healing to His people. There are stories in the Scriptures of people who had sickness for twelve, eighteen, thirty-seven, or more years. These should encourage you and offer you hope that God's able and willing to heal you. His heart toward you hasn't changed. He wants you to prosper and be in health.

Jesus is still in the business of bringing healing to His people.

In the pages that follow, may you be encouraged and strengthened in your faith to believe God for healing. My hope is for your spirit to fully grasp all that Christ has purchased for you and offers you today. I trust that you'll allow the Holy Spirit, who is our Teacher, to bring truth and revelation to you in a personal way. As you move from section to section of this book, I believe that you'll come to know Christ as not just a healer. It's my sincerest desire that you'll be able to profess, "Christ is my Healer!" In the end, may that confession and testimony propel you to minister the blessing of healing to others.

PART I

God's Provision
for Healing

CHAPTER 2

Making Us Whole

"May God himself, the God who makes everything holy and whole, make you holy and whole, put you together— spirit, soul, and body—and keep you fit for the coming of our Master Jesus Christ."

1 THESSALONIANS 5:23, MSG

First Thessalonians 5:23 is an important Scripture often used to identify the three distinct parts that comprise the essential nature of man—namely, spirit, soul, and body. Many people believe that the spirit and soul refer to the same entity. My response to that, however, is just as gold isn't silver and coffee isn't tea, I believe that *soul isn't spirit.*

Hebrews 4:12 tells us, "For the word of God is living and powerful, and sharper than any two-edged sword, piercing even to the *division* of soul and spirit . . ." (emphasis added). From this Scripture, we gather that the Word of God divides soul *and* spirit. Basically, man is a *spirit being* that has a soul, and that soul lives in his body.

Looking again at 1 Thessalonians 5:23, Paul lists the three elements of man in priority—first the spirit, then the soul, and lastly the body. With the *body,* we understand the *physical realm.* With the soul, we grasp hold of the *mental and emotional realms.* With the *spirit,* we're able to comprehend the *spiritual realm.*

In the fall of Adam and Eve, all three parts of the nature of man were affected. But the good news is that, in the redemption of man through Jesus Christ, all three areas were redeemed.

- For the spirit—sin, transgression, and iniquity are forgiven.
- For the soul—emotional and mental illness is healed.
- For the body—sickness is healed.

God's plan is always to bring wholeness to humanity—to the spirit, soul, and body. In Galilee, Jesus went about taking care of all three areas of man. We read:

> And Jesus went about all Galilee, *teaching* in their synagogues, *preaching* the gospel of the kingdom, and *healing* all kinds of sickness and all kinds of disease among the people. Then His fame went throughout all Syria; and they brought to Him all sick people who were afflicted with various diseases and torments, and those who were demon-possessed, epileptics, and paralytics; and He healed them (Matthew 4:23-24, emphasis added).

Here the Greek word for sickness is *malakia* (Strong, "Greek Dictionary of the New Testament," 46). It's a type of sickness that attacks the nerves, muscles, or the bones. You can live with the sickness, but the particular function of these systems of the body won't work. It's like having a leg but not being able to walk. It's like having a hand but not being able to grasp or hold. It's like having an eye but not being able to see. Many times, I've heard people say, "As long as you can live without it, God really doesn't care about healing it." *Wrong!* God is interested in making us whole—in healing our entire bodies. That's why He preached, taught, and healed! He preached to the spirit, taught the soul, and healed the body.

God made the body, and He sure knows how to heal it. God made the body to be healthy and well. We have a natural desire to be healthy in spirit, soul, and body. If we experience tension, anxiety, or fear, for example, we seek to be at peace. If we have any physical pain, we look to something to free us from the discomfort as soon as possible. Our normal reaction to sickness is to find a cure.

Even our bodies are equipped with natural healing properties that automatically function when something goes wrong. If we break one of our legs, the natural healing processes in our bodies will cause bones to grow together. A surgeon can set the bones in correct position, but he can't make them grow. No doctor can heal; he can only cooperate with the natural healing processes at work within our bodies.

A doctor can also help stimulate those processes through various kinds of treatment of medicine, surgery, etc., but he can't heal the wound. All the training that a doctor receives is to help him cooperate with the body's healing process. We need to see the relationship between God and doctors as one of cooperation, not competition. If healing is God's will for us, we should look at doctors and nurses as those who are cooperating with His divine will.

Commissioned for Wholeness

The English language is insufficient at times in expressing certain truths regarding sickness. In English, saying you're sick can mean you have anything from an annoying headache to something more serious like cancer or AIDS. This doesn't seem to do justice to these more serious cases. So it's helpful to look back at the original languages of the Bible—to look at the Greek or Hebrew— to get a proper understanding of the actual meaning.

Reading the English versions of the New Testament, in most of the healing accounts, the words for *sickness* and *disease* are more generalized also. We're not able to see from these words the gravity of the cases that Jesus healed. However, when we look to their original Greek words, we actually see the types of sicknesses that He healed.

It's quite interesting in Mark 16:18, when Jesus commissions the disciples to go and preach the Gospel and tells them that signs will follow the preaching, He commands them to lay hands on the sick. What kind of sick people was Jesus talking about? *Sick* in this verse is the Greek word *arrhostos* (Strong, "Greek Dictionary of the

New Testament," 16). *Arrhostos* is used when speaking of a person who is in bad health or critically ill, someone who falls in the category of an invalid. It's not talking about a person who simply feels under the weather with a cold or a headache but a person who is devastated by sickness. Someone who is an invalid can also mean someone who has lost consciousness and slipped into a coma. Such a one doesn't know where he is, what he is doing, or even who he is. He's completely incapacitated.

In Mark 6, Jesus entered into His home country, and many people came to him, but the Bible says He couldn't do much there because of their unbelief, only healing a few sick people. *Sick* here is the same word that Jesus used in Mark 16:18—to lay hands on the *sick*. It's the word *arrhostos*—meaning someone who is so critically ill that she can't exercise faith. This person's only means of healing is in the faith of someone else on her behalf. The reason I'm pointing out the word *arrhostos* is because Jesus is demonstrating to us in Mark 16:18 that we can lay hands on the worst sickness and believe for recovery. Praise God! Healing is God's plan!

The Bible records many cases where Jesus just went and started healing multitudes of people. One of those moments is found in Luke 4:40. It says, "When the sun was setting, all those who had any that were sick with various diseases brought them to Him; and He laid His hands on every one of them and healed them." The word for *disease* is the word, *nosos* (Strong, "Greek Dictionary of the New Testament," 50). *Nosos* means a terminal illness for which there is no natural cure. An example in our day might be AIDS. It's a *nosos*. As we see in Luke 4:40, Jesus healed various terminal illnesses—illnesses that were deadly like AIDS and cancer are deadly in this our day. Praise God! He has healed in history past and is healing in history today those diseases that have no natural cure.

> He has healed in history past and is healing in history today those diseases that have no natural cure.

Just think of the woman with the issue of blood. What an incredible testimony is hers! Let's look at it for a moment.

This woman, whose name we don't know, had a hemorrhage that was apparently destroying her for over twelve years. We can only imagine the pain and emotional pressure that sapped her strength day after day. Think of the many disappointments with the doctors and the financial loss that comes with the visits and medicine, and yet no improvement of health. Not only that, but there was one added burden: According to the Law, she was ceremonially unclean, which greatly restricted both her religious and her social life. (See Leviticus 15:19 for the law regarding women in her condition.) In bondage all around!

In spite of all the years of failure and frustration, she decided to still do something about her sickness. There is something to be said about a person who doesn't give up! She could have used any number of excuses to convince herself to stay away from Him. She might have said: "I'm not important enough to ask Jesus for help!" She might have concluded, "Look, He's going with Jairus, so I won't bother Him now." She could have argued that nothing else had helped her, so why try again. She may have even thought that it wasn't right to come to Jesus as a last resort, after visiting all those other physicians. However, she put aside all arguments and excuses and came by faith to Jesus. She pushed through the crowds that were following Him and confessed, "'If only I may touch His clothes, I shall be made well'" (Mark 5:28). She touched His clothes, and her faith brought her wholeness.

> . . . she put aside all arguments and excuses and came by faith to Jesus. She pushed through the crowds . . .

The interesting thing that I notice about this particular healing is that the King James Version calls her sickness a plague—"And straightway the fountain of her blood was dried up; and she felt in her body that she was healed of that *plague*" (Mark 5:29, emphasis added). The Greek word for plague is *mastix* (Strong, "Greek Dictionary of the New Testament," 46). It has its roots in the whole idea of torture. *Torture* and *plague* often were used interchangeably.

In those days, torture looked something like this: A victim was tied to a post, and then a torturer would come with a whip and strike the person until the point of death. He would then be taken and left in a cell to heal. Just about the time he felt life was normal again and healing had taken place, he was again taken to the post and whipped. This kept happening over and over again, every time bringing him to the point of death but never killing him. This was the definition of torture. Now, let's think of the torture this woman received from her sickness for twelve years. Twelve years, this pattern of sickness was destroying her. It repeatedly whipped her again and again. It kept recurring to the point of death.

There are many whose sickness is like a plague. It keeps recurring seasonally or eventfully in life-patterns of headaches, of asthma attacks, of cold, of flu, of seizures, etc. Whatever the case, I want to assure you that if Jesus healed plagues 2,000 years ago, then He is still healing people of plagues today, making them whole in their spirits, souls, and bodies as He did the woman with the issue of blood and the leper of Matthew 8.

CHAPTER 3

Salvation in Its Entirety

*"When He had come down from the mountain,
great multitudes followed Him. And behold, a leper came
and worshiped Him, saying, 'Lord, if You are willing,
You can make me clean.' Then Jesus put out His hand
and touched him, saying, 'I am willing; be cleansed.'"
Immediately his leprosy was cleansed."*

MATTHEW 8:1-3

On one particular day, as Jesus was coming down the
mountain where He had just spent days teaching thousands of people the Beatitudes or "attitudes to be," a
leper decided to approach Him. This story of the leper is found in
three different places in Scripture—Matthew 8:1-3, Mark 1:40-
42, and Luke 5:12-13. This is Jesus' first recorded healing of an
individual. Of course, up until this time many were healed, but
this story is the first record of an individual being healed.

I find it interesting that the first recorded healing would
involve a leper because leprosy was probably the worst possible
sickness one could have during the time of Christ. Leprosy was an
incurable disease. Praise Jesus! He healed leprosy demonstrating
that He is able to heal the worst of sicknesses! He "*is* the same yes-
terday, today, and forever" (Hebrews 13:8). To Him, healing leprosy is no different than healing a cold or a cough. All sickness was
paid for by the stripes He received upon His back.

We also need to understand how leprosy was viewed in the

Bible. It not only was known as a sickness, but it served as a type or a symbol of sin. This is very important to understand because it's further evidence of what Christ accomplished for us on the cross. He paid the price for the forgiveness of our sins *and* for the healing of our bodies. His work on the cross gave us the whole package for our cleansing and healing.

Leviticus 14 talks about how a person who might have leprosy was to be made clean. This chapter addresses leprosy in the body of an individual and also in a house. In verse 19, we read the priest actually offered an offering for the leprous person. In fact, the offering required was a sin offering. So the leper would receive healing for his leprosy *and* forgiveness for his sin. The principles in the Bible concerning healing are as simple as that of receiving forgiveness of sin and coming into new birth.

All of this was a part of the *atonement* in the Old Testament. The atonement of that time was an event scheduled once a year for offering sacrifices of animals to cover the sins of people for that year. It was a type of what Jesus as the Lamb of God would do on the cross. So atonement was the price paid for sin, death, shame, and sickness. In the Old Testament, the atonement was only a covering of sin, but what Jesus did on the cross permanently broke the power of sin over our lives once and for all.

The Work of Salvation

Isaiah 53 records the most detailed and life-giving prophecies about the work of salvation upon the cross. Let's look at the first part of this prophecy that came to pass in the work of redemption.

Isaiah 53:1 reads, "Who has believed our report? And to whom has the arm of the Lord been revealed?" The *report* refers to the rest of the verses. *The arm of the Lord* refers to salvation. Another Scripture in Isaiah says, "The arm of the Lord is not too short to save" (59:1, NIV). Praise God! Jesus' arms reached out to each one of us to bring us into the family of God.

The next two verses of Isaiah 53 read:

For He shall grow up before Him as a tender plant, and as a root out of dry ground. He has no form or comeliness; and when we see Him, there is no beauty that we should desire Him. He is despised and rejected by men, a Man of sorrows and acquainted with grief. And we hid, as it were, our faces from Him; He was despised, and we did not esteem Him (vv. 2-3).

A root out of dry ground is an odd phrase, for what root can grow out of ground that is without water? It seems contrary to nature. In the same manner, Jesus was born of a virgin. He had a supernatural birth.

Now, we come to the beautiful picture portrayed here of our Savior and His efficacious work on Calvary—"Surely He has borne our griefs. And carried our sorrows; yet we esteemed Him stricken, smitten by God, and afflicted. But He was wounded for our transgressions, He was bruised for our iniquities; the chastisement for our peace was upon Him, and by His stripes we are healed" (Isaiah 53:4-5).

In the Hebrew language, the word *sorrows* is *makôb*, meaning physical pain (Strong, "Hebrew and Chaldee Dictionary," 66). *Grief* here is *choliy*, meaning sickness and disease (Strong, "Hebrew and Chaldee Dictionary," 39). The gospel writer says it more appropriately in Matthew 8:17—"that it might be fulfilled which was spoken by Isaiah the prophet, saying: *He Himself took our infirmities and bore our sicknesses.*" Simon Peter also picks this up and says in 1 Peter 2:24, ". . . by whose stripes you were healed." Peter doesn't speak of healing as something that was going to happen in the future. Rather he speaks in past tense. He speaks of a fact already accomplished. It's done. It's finished!

> It's totally inconsistent to say that Jesus died for our sins without also saying that He died for our sicknesses.

In Christ's work of atonement, His blood was shed for our sins, and He received the stripes on His body for our healing. It's totally inconsistent to say that Jesus died for our sins without also saying that He died for our sicknesses. It's equally inconsistent to claim that forgiveness is available for all, but healing is only for some.

Looking back at the New Testament healing of the leper, we read that Jesus told him to go show himself to the priest. According to the Law, the priest was to offer sacrifices for the leper so that he could be pronounced clean. In the book of Leviticus, we find that in other cases, when people came to the priest, they took with them a sacrifice, but for the leper the priest had to give the sacrifice. It's the same way for us, for our healing. Jesus, our Priest, gave the sacrifice by offering Himself as the Lamb. Our *leprosy*, albeit sin or sickness, was washed away by Christ's atoning blood. We're no longer contaminated by sin or sickness. We've been declared clean *and* healed!

In the Old Testament, we find other types and shadows of many truths that were fulfilled in the life of Jesus. Let's look at two other events foreshadowing the work of Christ's atonement on the cross.

Passover in Egypt

All around the world, people are going crazy with diets. They're eating organic foods and avoiding others that will help keep the body healthy and strong. Well, we have such a meal in the Scriptures. We eat this meal, and it promises life and health. This meal is known as the Passover meal because it's eaten at the time of the festival of Passover.

The Passover marked a new beginning for the Jews and bound them together as a nation. When the Lord liberates us from bondage and we're born again, a new day dawns, and we experience the beginning of our new lives.

In the Old Testament, the Jewish nation had two calendars, a civil calendar that began in our September or October, and a religious calendar that began in our March or April. New Year's Day in the civil year (*Rosh Hashanah*—"beginning of the year") fell in the seventh month of the religious calendar and ushered in the special events in the month of Tishri—namely, the Feast of Trumpets, the Day of Atonement, and the Feast of Tabernacles. But Passover marked the beginning of the religious year, and at Passover, the focus was and is on the lamb. Of course, this pointed to Jesus as being the Lamb. The origin of this feast was when the Israelites were delivered from Egypt.

In the Scriptures, the whole story of the Israelites leaving Egypt, going through the wilderness, and coming to the Promised Land was symbolic of salvation—the same salvation released through the work of the cross. So in the story, we can surmise that Egypt represents sin and bondage. Pharaoh represents Satan, and Moses is a type of Christ, the Deliverer. The wilderness, then, stands for training for life, while the Promised Land symbolizes a place of reward and inheritance that we receive in Christ Jesus.

The story of the Passover is detailed for us in Exodus 12. When time came for the deliverance of the nation of Israel out of Egypt, the *house of bondage*, God gave Moses instructions concerning the means of deliverance. It was the message of the Passover lamb.

The head of each household was told to take the lamb of the first year without spot or blemish. This is a perfect representation of Christ. Jesus was the perfect sacrifice. He was without sin. People like Pilate, Herod, the centurion, and even the repentant thief on the cross acknowledged Jesus as the Lamb without any spot or blemish.

> **Jesus isn't just a Savior, but *our Savior.***

On the tenth day of the month until the fourteenth day, the lamb was to be with the family. The reason for this is the family would get familiar with the lamb so that it wasn't just any lamb, but *their* lamb. In the same manner, Jesus isn't just a Savior, but *our Savior*. Exodus 12 records three different references to the lamb—verse three has *a lamb*, verse four uses *the lamb*, and finally, verse five reads *your lamb*. Here, we can see the deepening relationship between the lamb and its respective family.

On the fourteenth day at nine o'clock in the morning, the head of the household would take the lamb and place his hand on it, symbolically placing the sins of the household onto it. Then at three o'clock in the afternoon, the throat of the lamb was cut. The blood that was shed then was applied to the lintel and doorpost of the house using a hyssop. For us today, our faith represents the hyssop that we use to apply the blood of Jesus to our lives.

The household itself was to feast upon the body of the lamb. They were to eat with:

- Their loins girded (Exodus 12:11; Ephesians 6:14; 1 Peter 1:13).
- Their shoes on their feet (Exodus 12:11; Ephesians 6:15).
- Their staffs in their hands (Exodus 12:11; Hebrews 11:13).
- Bitter herbs and unleavened bread (Exodus 12:8).
- Speed, ensuring the dough had no time to leaven (Exodus 12:11; Hebrews 11:13).

The head, legs, and purtenence were to be fed upon. This, then, signifies the believer's feeding on Christ's mind (the head), walk (legs), and inward motives and the affections (inward parts).

A person had to be circumcised to eat the Passover (Exodus 12:43-51). A stranger wasn't to eat of it. A foreigner wasn't to eat of it. A hired servant wasn't to eat of it. Parallel to the New Testament, only a person that has his heart circumcised, who has repented of his sins and accepted Jesus into his heart, is able to enjoy the benefits of the Lord's Supper. "In Christ," we're no longer foreigners or strangers.

Then at midnight, the death angel would pass through Israel, and every house that didn't have the token of the blood on the doorpost and lintel would suffer judgment and death. The angel would *pass over* the house with the blood applied.

As we continue reading the story, we find that judgment fell on the Egyptians with the death of their firstborn children and beasts. Pharaoh called for Moses and Aaron and told them to get out of Egypt immediately. In their haste to get rid of the Israelites, they were spoiled. The Israelites took from the Egyptians jewels of gold, silver, raiment, and anything else required. They actually were instructed to ask their Egyptian neighbors for these items, and their neighbors gave them of their stuff. It was Israel's payday for many years of work and slavery. In due time, the Israelites would give of their substance to build the tabernacle of the Lord. Looking again to the New Testament type, we recognize that Christ spoiled principalities and powers in His triumph on the cross and His *exodus,* and the believing church partakes of these spoils won through His death (Colossians 2:10-15).

Now let's connect this whole story with what God says in Psalm 105:37—"He also brought them out with silver and gold, and there was none feeble among His tribes." Can you imagine millions of Israelites without a feeble one among them? What a miracle! What a Healer! Not only was the Passover a type of dealing with sin but also sickness. No one had fever. No one had a tumor. No one was carried on a stretcher. No one left on crutches.

> **Jesus, the Lamb of God, took away our sin and our sickness.**

Again, this was a type of the work of salvation on the cross. Jesus, the Lamb of God, took away our sin and our sickness. This was such a significant event that they were commanded to keep the Passover continually as a memorial (Exodus 12:14).

For us in the New Testament, the ordinance of the Lord's Supper replaces the Passover Feast. The Lord's Supper is a memorial feast for He asks us to "'do this in remembrance of'" Him (Matthew 26:26-28). I believe, as the children of Israel *look forward* to the work of the cross, we *look back* to the work of the cross. And every time we do, we can choose to receive the benefits of the work of salvation in its entirety!

We must keep in mind that not only have we been delivered from being slaves to sin and sickness, but the work of the cross has "translated *us* into the kingdom of his dear Son" (Colossians 1:13, KJV) and made us "a new creation" in Christ Jesus (2 Corinthians 5:17). The fallen nature of the first Adam came with sickness and could be influenced by it, but the nature of God, which you have now received, came with life. The Greek word for this life is *zoe* (Strong, "Greek Dictionary of the New Testament," 35). The moment you were born again, *zoe*, or the very nature of God, moved inside your spirit.

Zoe affects our development as Christians. This new life of God in us destroys our sin nature and expels the darkness in our lives. The life of God in us will enable us to walk in God's ways and obey His commandments. If we're willing to allow the new spirit within us, which is born of the Spirit of God, to dominate us rather than live by our flesh, we'll develop in our walk with the Lord and grow in the things of God. In Ezekiel 36:26-27, God says, "'A new heart also will I give you, and a new spirit will I put within you: and I will take away the stony heart out of your flesh, and I will give you a heart of flesh. And I will put my spirit within you, and cause you to walk in my statutes, and ye shall keep my judgments, and do them'" (KJV).

Now, let's look at the other event that foreshadows Christ's work of salvation.

The Serpent on the Pole

The Israelites were delivered out of Egypt—at least their bodies were; their minds and hearts were still back in the land of bondage. They came out, and from the day they hit the wilderness, they complained. They griped about Moses. They didn't like his leadership. They moaned and groaned about the wilderness. They didn't like their circumstances. They griped about the food. They wanted to go back to the low-fat, low-cholesterol diet of Egypt, where they had leeks and onions. They had what we would crudely call diarrhea of the tongue—constant grumbling and complaining. They were like kids on a long trip. They wanted to stop at every fast-food joint along the way, and yet they wanted to already be at their final destination. And they kept at it and kept at it until God got sick of it. So He sent snakes into the camp—poisonous snakes.

According to the encyclopedia, there are between 2,500 and 3,000 different varieties of snakes crawling around the planet, and most of them serve some good purpose. They eat rodents like mice and rats. But for some reason, whenever we think of snakes, we always think of bad snakes—like copperheads, rattlers, vipers, cobras, or pythons. And those bad snakes give the good snakes a bad name, so to speak. Personally, whatever their purpose, I don't like snakes. I can't stand the sight of one. Whatever types of snakes were released among the Israelites, those snakes bit the people. It was like fire going through their bodies, and the bites for some were fatal. The Israelites got the message. They turned to Moses and asked him to go to God and do something (Numbers 21:6-7).

The snakes that had caused death were going to be counteracted by a bronze snake that would bring life . . .

And God said to Moses, "'Make a fiery serpent, and set it on a pole; and it shall be that everyone who is bitten, when he looks at it, shall live'" (Numbers 21:8). You have to admit, that's a strange way to get rid of snakebite. The snakes that had caused death were going to be counteracted by a bronze snake that would bring life (Numbers 21:9). The snakes that were the emblems of a curse were thwarted by a bronze snake that became the emblem of God's blessing. The snakes that were hated were countermanded by that bronze snake that was the blessing of God. It was a good snake—a real good snake.

The serpent on the pole was symbolic of Jesus being lifted up and nailed to the cross.

"And as Moses lifted up the serpent in the wilderness, even so must the Son of Man be lifted up, that whoever believes in Him should not perish but have eternal life. For God so loved the world that He gave His only begotten Son, that whoever believes in Him should not perish but have everlasting life. For God did not send His Son into the world to condemn the world, but that the world through Him might be saved" (John 3:14-17).

Jesus did not only bear the curse, He *became* the curse as we read in Galatians 3:13—"Christ has redeemed us from the curse of the law, having become a curse for us (for it is written, *'Cursed is everyone who hangs on a tree'*)."

The Israelites had to look in faith to the bronze serpent so that they could be forgiven of the sin and be healed of the snakebite. *The Amplified Bible* expands the word *look* to mean, "attentively, expectantly, with a steady and absorbing gaze." In the same manner, we have to learn to receive our healing by becoming absorbed with Christ, our Healer!

> It's amazing that many believe in this story in the Bible but still don't believe in healing today.

It's amazing that many believe in this story in the Bible but still don't believe in healing today. What an incongruent belief system is theirs! It's as if the antitype had power to heal, and Jesus Christ, to whom the reality the type points, shouldn't have that power. Listen, if the antitype had power and if healing was released in the Old Testament, how much more is it available today for you and me who are living in the realm of grace that came through Jesus. Look to Christ as your healer.

St. Francis of Assisi is said to have contemplated on the cross of Christ so much, preached it so much, and talked so much about it that he said to the people, "When I die open my body, and you'll find the very print of the cross on my heart." After he died, they allegedly opened his body and found it to be so—the imprint of the cross was right on his physical heart (Oyakhilome 48). We should look so much to Christ that His imprint is all over our lives.

On the Island of Melita, the apostle Paul was bitten by a viper as he made a fire. Everyone around him expected him to swell and die soon. Paul just shook off the viper into the fire, and no harm came to him (Acts 28:1-6). Paul was very much conscious of who was inside him, ". . . Christ in [him], the hope of glory."

In 2 Kings 18, in the time of King Hezekiah, we find that the people were using the serpent on the pole as an object of worship.

The bronze serpent on a pole was a symbol pointing ahead to the fullness of time when Jesus would come and fulfill all the types, shadows, and other symbols of the Old Testament. Jesus fulfilled the bronze serpent typology. Therefore, at anytime it is wrong to worship the serpent on the pole. It was never intended for worship. It was a onetime event to bring reconciliation and healing to the children of Israel in the wilderness.

Likewise, we need to keep in mind that we don't worship the symbol of the cross either. The cross itself doesn't save us, but faith in Christ and His work on the cross do. We can't look to the cross for our redemption. We must believe in the work of salvation on the cross. I'm not implying that we shouldn't use crosses or put them on the top of our church buildings. I'm merely highlighting the fact that we can use the cross as a memory to remind us of what Jesus did, but we must keep clear of worshiping the cross itself.

Salvation occurs the moment we embrace by faith all that Jesus accomplished on the cross, in the tomb, in the resurrection, and in the ascension. Through Him, we're redeemed back to God our Father and have received the "Spirit of adoption by whom we cry out 'Abba, Father'" (Romans 8:15).

Adopted into His Family

The greatest thing I know about God is that He is our Father. The next best thing is that He is full of love.

The apostle John joyfully proclaims, "Behold what manner of love the Father has bestowed on us, that we should be called children of God!" (1 John 3:1). And this love caused the Father to send His only Son to earth to restore humanity to Himself. Love led Jesus to obey His Father and leave heaven to come and live among us. Jesus is Love personified. The gospels of Matthew, Mark, Luke, and John record the amazing and astounding stories of His great love. When we read the signs and wonders that are recorded therein, we conclude that only Love can make a miracle. Only Love can bring healing to a sick person. Only Love can restore a family.

The Holy Spirit pours the love of God into our hearts (Romans 5:5). This love redeems us from the world of darkness, adopts us, and makes us family. Speaking of this, I'm reminded of a story about two new boys who enrolled in Sunday school. In order to register, the superintendent asked their ages and birthdays. The bolder of the two said, "We're both seven. My birthday is April 8, 2003, and my brother's is April 20, 2003."

"But that's impossible!" answered the superintendent.

"No, it's not," answered the quieter brother. "One of us is adopted."

"Which one?" asked the superintendent, blurting out her question before she could stop herself.

The boys looked at each other and smiled, and the bolder one said to the superintendent, "We asked Dad a while ago, but he just said he loved us both, and he couldn't remember any more which one was adopted" (*10,000 Sermon* "Acceptance —God's Love").

We need to realize that the way the Father loves Jesus is the way the Father loves you and me.

In Roman 8:16-17, Paul writes, "We are children of God and if children, then heirs—heirs of God and joint heirs with Christ." Paul uses the image of adoption when speaking of our relationship with God in Christ. By our faith in Christ, we become his adopted brothers and sisters—adopted sons and daughters of God. As fully adopted and accepted children, we share the same inheritance as the begotten Son, Jesus. No wonder all creation waits eagerly for the full revealing and adoption to happen! We need to realize that the way the Father loves Jesus is the way the Father loves you and me. The way the Father treats Jesus is the way He will treat you and me. We're family.

This same God who is full of love is also very approachable. The Bible says in John 6:37 that he who comes to Jesus, He "'will by no means cast out.'" As a matter of fact, when we approach God, we need to approach with boldness even when we have sin in our lives. Sin will tempt us to *run away from* God, but we need to *run to* God because He is the only one who can help us. We need to simply come and surrender to Him, for He is our every provision. As the writer of Hebrews encourages us, "Let us therefore come boldly to the throne of grace, that we may obtain mercy and find grace to help in time of need" (4:16). The following "Amazon Story" demonstrates how often we miss God's help:

> The Amazon River is the largest river in the world. The mouth is 90 miles across. There is enough water to exceed the combined flow of the Yangtze, Mississippi, and Nile Rivers. So much water comes from the Amazon that they can detect its currents 200 miles out in the Atlantic Ocean. One irony of ancient navigation is that sailors in ancient times died for lack of water . . . caught in windless waters of the South Atlantic. They were adrift, helpless, dying of thirst. Sometimes other ships from South America who knew the area would come alongside and call out, "What is your problem?" And they would exclaim, "Can you spare us some water? Our sailors are dying of thirst!" And from the other ship would come the cry, "Just lower your buckets. You are in the mouth of the mighty Amazon River." The irony of ancient Israel and the tragedy around us today is that God, the fountain of living water, is right here; we simply need to humble ourselves and bow before Him and drink of living water that brings healing life (Hewett 242).

When we read the life of Jesus recorded in the Gospels, we find that prostitutes felt comfortable to approach Him, businessmen felt comfortable to go up to Him, children felt comfortable to draw near to Him, rich people felt comfortable to come to Him, and rulers even felt comfortable to approach Jesus. When I look at the church today, how different we've become. The church today seems to stay at a "safe" distance, but we all need to feel safest when we're closest to Him. Furthermore, we have to believe that He has everything we need; He's the solution to our every problem.

Praise God! Healing is part of the whole package of salvation. Our sins are forgiven by the blood of Jesus, and we can receive healing for our physical bodies because of the stripes Jesus received. The leper, who represents both the sinner and sick, found wholeness coming to Jesus. In the following chapter, we'll see the leper's approach to asking Jesus to heal him.

CHAPTER 4

Worship: The Healing Posture

"'And behold, a leper came and worshiped Him . . .'"
MATTHEW 8:2

Kinesics? Ever heard of it? I would never heard the word before until recently my friend, Johnny Lever, who is a famous actor and comedian in the nation of India, was interviewed for a magazine. In the article, the interviewer wrote so much about his communicating through his facial expressions and body. It was the first time I heard the word *kinesics*.

Kinesics is the study of nonverbal communication or body language. It's the idea that people communicate not just with words, but with facial expressions, gestures, stances, movements, and even postures. If we talk to a man who is constantly looking around, we're tempted to suspect he's not listening. Whether we realize it or not, we're attentive to the nonverbal cues around us.

The Scriptures communicate such body language. Bowing, kneeling, begging, eyeing—these are all forms of nonverbal communication. But just what do these cues say to us? What, for example, does it mean when we read someone was bowing? Well, for one thing, bowing communicates humility or humiliation; it says, "I'm not worthy to stand in the presence of this person." Who deserves that kind of treatment? The Bible says Jesus Christ does.

In the New Testament all kinds of people bow low before Jesus —lepers, demon-possessed people, and frightened disciples who watch Jesus calm a storm on command. Each time they bow before Him, they communicate something important about who Jesus is and who they are. Bowing signifies Jesus Christ is worthy of worship. He's worthy for all to bow before Him, not just with our bodies, but with our minds, our hearts, and our wills in surrender to Him.

True biblical worship so satisfies our total personality that we don't have to shop around for man-made substitutes. William Temple made this clear in his masterful definition of worship:

> For worship is the submission of all our nature to God. It is the quickening of conscience by His holiness; the nourishment of mind with His truth; the purifying of imagination by His beauty; the opening of the heart to His love; the surrender of will to His purpose—and all of this gathered up in adoration, the most selfless emotion of which our nature is capable and therefore the chief remedy for that self-centeredness which is our original sin and the source of all actual sin (Wiersbe 119).

When we look, then, at the leper in Matthew 8, we see he approached Jesus and first worshiped Him even though there was a crowd of people. Depending on which Scripture reference or Bible translation we read, there are various phrases used to describe the leper's worship. According to these, the leper *came and knelt before him, bowed down before him, humbled himself before Jesus,* etc. All these reveal the condition of his heart. Remember, Jesus always focused on the condition of the heart. At that moment, people probably looked at the outward clothes or covering this leper had on and began to judge him, but Jesus looked past all that and saw his heart.

In times past, lepers lived separately from the rest of society, mostly outside the city, and they had to wear clothes of mourning and covering. If by any chance a person came near a leper, the leper had to warn the individual by shouting, "Unclean!" Nevertheless, the leper of our story stepped out in front of the crowds and came to Jesus. He knelt down in submission to Christ.

The psalmist encourages us is Psalm 95:6-7, "Oh come, let us worship and bow down; let us kneel before the Lord our Maker. For He *is* our God, and we *are* the people of His pasture, and the sheep of His hand." The *bowing* in this verse isn't just a physical act, but an act of inward submission to someone greater. It's an act of honor. Napoleon Bonaparte probably gave one of the best explanations of the difference between honoring a man and worshiping God: "If Socrates would enter the room, we should rise and do him honor," Bonaparte said, "but if Jesus Christ came into the room, we should fall down on our knees and worship him" (Wiersbe 180). I believe the leper bowed down because he recognized that Jesus was the Messiah. Jesus was indeed the Shepherd, and he was the sheep.

Worship Defined

Worship is the attitude of the heart that affects our whole being. Worship involves our whole body. The contents of our hearts will always be displayed through our body. The majority of the Scriptures dealing with worship describe a bodily attitude. These Scriptures depict worship as that of bowing, kneeling, humbling, and falling prostrate or face to the ground.

We can say that worship is the dethronement of ourselves and the enthronement of God. Joshua understood this very well for it says in Joshua 5:13-15—

And then this, while Joshua was there near Jericho: he looked up and saw right in front of him a man standing, holding his drawn sword. Joshua stepped up to him and said, "Whose side are you on—ours or our enemies?" He said, "Neither. I'm commander of God's army. I've just arrived." Joshua fell, face to the ground, and worshiped. He asked, "What orders does my Master have for his servant?" God's army commander ordered Joshua, "Take your

sandals off your feet. The place you are standing is holy."
Joshua did it (MSG).

Many times when people hear the word, *worship,* they are accustomed to thinking of slow-paced songs, music, etc. I've even heard some say ignorantly that praise is singing fast songs and worship is singing slow songs. Praise, songs, and music are only a part of worship. Worship is making a choice to give honor, value, respect, and credit to God. In Luke 7:36-50, a woman with an alabaster box came near Jesus, knelt down, and worshiped him. She had no instruments or songs, yet she loved much. We can worship with music, praise, and songs, but worship isn't limited to that.

There are many times I've had sickness and trials in my life when I began to receive healing just by worshiping God. Songs are not the main aspect of worship. Songs are part of the mode of worship. Worship isn't about any particular place where spiritual activities are going on. The focus of worship is always Jesus. The Samaritan woman and Jesus had this discussion in John 4:20-24—

"Well, tell me this: Our ancestors worshiped God at this mountain, but you Jews insist that Jerusalem is the only place for worship, right?" "Believe me, woman, the time is coming when you Samaritans will worship the Father neither here at this mountain nor there in Jerusalem. You worship guessing in the dark; we Jews worship in the clear light of day. God's way of salvation is made available through the Jews. But the time is coming—it has, in fact, come—when what you're called will not matter and where you go to worship will not matter. It's who you are and the way you live that count before God. Your worship must engage your spirit in the pursuit of truth. That's the kind of people the Father is out looking for: those who are simply and honestly *themselves* before him in their worship. God is sheer being itself—Spirit. Those who worship him must do it out of their very being, their spirits, their true selves, in adoration" (MSG).

In times of my personal worship to God, or even when I'm in a meeting where I'm encouraging and leading people in worship, I'm always drawn to the encounter of Isaiah. I believe worship is an encounter. Every time we worship the Lord, we can have an encounter with God. Even as the leper worshiped God, he had an encounter with Him. An encounter occurs when God intentionally meets with you, in a time of great personal need, through unexpected circumstances, telling you something about Himself. You learn something about yourself. It prepares you for a specific task. Many times, we don't fully understand all the elements of what happened in that moment, but as time goes on, we see the purposes of God unfolding, and we begin to realize the power of that encounter.

As we look at this event, I want to affirm the fact that worship isn't just an event that happens off and on in our lives. According to the Scripture, worship is a lifestyle for the believer. When I'm referring to worship in this chapter, I'm not dealing with the lifestyle of worship, but those pivotal moments in our lives when we have an encounter with God that brings about a blessing from the Lord.

Let's look at one such encounter that Isaiah had in the sixth chapter of the book bearing his name. I believe the encounter can be outlined in three stages—upward look, inward look, and outward expression. Each of these stages can be experienced through worship. Let's look at them.

Upward Look

According to Isaiah 6, we read it was the year King Uzziah died and Isaiah saw the Lord. One thing that was the highlight of King Uzziah's life was his pride, and that pride led to his having leprosy. The correlation is that pride hinders us from seeing God. You might say that King Uzziah had pride, not Isaiah. That's right! But the reason I believe this verse begins this way is to let us know that, during the reign of Uzziah, everything was dominated by him. As he was the leader, he was even the obstacle keeping others from encountering God. Many times when we have wrong associations, habits, and pride, they become blockages to our having an encounter with God. One thing initially blocking the leper in Matthew 8 was that people had set him aside from the society, but he decided to look past all that and approach Jesus.

Isaiah saw the Lord sitting on a throne, high and lifted up, and the train of His robe filled the temple. John 12:41 confirms that Isaiah saw Jesus—"These things Isaiah said when he saw His glory and spoke of Him." This picture is a picture of Jesus as King. So one aspect of worship is to have an upward look and acknowledge Jesus as King, Jesus as Lord, and Jesus as the Holy One.

Isaiah 6:2-3 tells us that Isaiah saw angels also in the presence of God, and he noticed the attitude of their worship. The seraphim used a pair of wings to cover their faces, and the second pair to cover their feet, and the third pair to fly as they cried to one another, "'Holy, holy, holy is the Lord of hosts.'" It's interesting that the seraphim used more wings to worship than they did to fly.

Flying is symbolic of our service to the Lord. By using the term *service*, I also mean ministry. Furthermore, I believe that any ministry or service should be united in worship. I believe every time the word *holy* is used, it's referring to each person of the Godhead. Holy is God the Father; Holy is God the Son—Jesus; and Holy is God the Spirit. Worship always keeps us in touch with the beauty of God's holiness.

Inward Look

The second thing that happens is that Isaiah gets an inward look. This is of utmost important. As we see the Lord, we need to see ourselves in the light of God. Isaiah 6:5-8 gives us a clear picture—

"Woe is me, for I *am* undone! Because I *am* a man of unclean lips, and I dwell in the midst of a people of unclean

lips; for my eyes have seen the King, the LORD of hosts."
Then one of the seraphim flew to me, having in his hand
a live coal *which* he had taken with the tongs from the altar.
And he touched my mouth *with it*, and said: "Behold, this
has touched your lips; your iniquity is taken away, and
your sin purged."

I want us to keep in mind that this man Isaiah was a godly
man. He loved and served the Lord, but coming into the presence
of God, this holy man was made aware of his own sin and unworthiness. We often feel like Isaiah—*I don't have it together*, we think.
Having seen who God is, how can I expect Him to take me seriously?
we wonder. God isn't out to condemn us and make us feel like out-
casts, rather He wants to clean us up and reveal to us the treasure
He's invested in us.

God calls us to worship in His presence, expecting us to join
with the angels, crying out, "Holy, holy, holy!" In this act, His being
and nature begin to be transferred into our lives. Those things that
are in line with His plans begin to be restored back into our lives.

I believe every encounter with God begins to change and trans-
form us. God doesn't reveal anything about Himself, unless He's
revealing to restore something that we've lost. God's desire is that
we constantly change more and more into His image.

In Matthew 16, we have a wonderful example of transforma-
tion taking place as a disciple gets revelation of Jesus and himself.
At a moment's notice, Jesus asks His disciples, "'Who do men say
that I, the Son of Man, am?'" (v. 13). Some answered by saying
others said He was John the Baptist, and some said Elijah (v. 14).
But when Jesus asked, "'Who do you say that I am?'" (v. 15), Simon
said, "'You are the Christ, the Son of the living God'" (v. 16). You
see, he got a revelation of Jesus by the Holy Spirit. Even Jesus said,
"'Blessed are you, Simon Bar-Jonah, for flesh and blood has not
revealed *this* to you, but My Father who is in heaven'" (v. 17).

Jesus didn't leave it there; He turned to him and said, "'. . . you are Peter'" (Matthew 16:18). You see, Simon simply meant a small little pebble, but now Jesus was giving him a revelation about him, saying to Simon, "You are not a pebble, but a solid rock." You see, every revelation of God restores something that we need to have. Even in the encounter of Isaiah, God was restoring holiness back to Isaiah.

> You see, every revelation of God restores something that we need to have.

Isaiah, standing in the presence of God, was transformed as the angel sent by God came with a live coal in his hands and touched the lips of Isaiah and made him clean. Had he felt that his hands were unclean, the Lord would probably have touched his hands. Any area in our lives that God is putting His finger on isn't meant to expose and condemn us but to restore and heal us.

The live coal speaks of fire. Fire is the element used to bring about healing and restoration. What does fire do?

Fire refines us. It burns out everything that is unclean and polishes us with the holiness of God. It refines us and makes us people who can receive from God. We see this in Malachi 3:3—"He will sit as a refiner and a purifier of silver; He will purify the sons of Levi, and purge them as gold and silver, that they may offer to the LORD an offering in righteousness.'"

Fire consumes. Those things that never seem to go away always come up and produce guilt in our lives, but God's able to completely destroy them. Even our attempts at pleasing God sometimes are self-serving in the end, and in turn, they become chords of failure that hold us back from approaching Him. As Psalm 97:3 says, "Fire goes before him and consumes his foes on every side" (NIV).

Fire melts. Our hard, metal-jacket protected hearts are made soft. Our emotions are made pure. How is this accomplished? By the work of the Holy Spirit. John the Baptist said:

> "I baptize you with water for repentance. But after me will come one who is more powerful than I, whose sandals I am not fit to carry. He will baptize you with the Holy Spirit

and with fire. His winnowing fork is in his hand, and he will clear his threshing floor, gathering his wheat into the barn and burning up the chaff with unquenchable fire" (Matthew 3:11-12, NIV).

Fire warms. Lost passion is restored. A heart song is restored. The joy of salvation is restored. There is a longing to seek God's face before His hand. The disciples tarried in the Upper Room. When, suddenly, "a sound like the blowing of a violent wind came from heaven and filled the whole house where they were sitting. They saw what seemed to be tongues of fire that separated and came to rest on each of them. All of them were filled with the Holy Spirit and began to speak in other tongues as the Spirit enabled them" (Acts 2:2-4, NIV).

Fire ignites. Those things that are dead because of failure, frustration, and defeat are made alive again. Your prayer life comes alive. "Oh, that you would rend the heavens and come down, that the mountains would tremble before you! As when fire sets twigs ablaze and causes water to boil, come down to make your name known to your enemies and cause the nations to quake before you!" (Isaiah 64:1-2, NIV).

Every time we get an upward look, we also need to expect an inward look. God wants to do something *in* us. God wants to do something *for* us. God wants to deposit things in us that are lacking. Maybe we need grace in certain areas. Maybe we need healing. Maybe we have heavy burdens. Whatever the case, God wants to work in our lives.

Isaiah was given an inward look to advance him in life. How I pray that God keeps giving me an inward look and keeps filling me with those things that are lacking—that I may bring full glory and honor to His name. There is power in worship. Whatever your need is, approach God in worship, bowing down before Him, bringing your life in total submission to His Lordship.

Outward Expression

The third part of the encounter is recorded in Isaiah 6:8. It reads, "Also I heard the voice of the LORD, saying: 'Whom shall I send, and who will go for Us?' Then I said, 'Here *am* I! Send me.'" God touched Isaiah for service. I believe as we worship God, God will honor us by using us to serve Him and serve His ministry.

Matthew 4 records the time when Satan showed up to tempt Jesus to bow down and worship him. Matthew 4:10 gives us Jesus' response. Let's look at it in *The Message* Bible translation—"Jesus' refusal was curt: 'Beat it, Satan!' He backed his rebuke with a third quotation from Deuteronomy: 'Worship the Lord your God, and only him. Serve him with absolute single-heartedness.'"

The Scriptures always see service in the context of worship, as if to say that any service that does not honor God is useless. A believer who has had an upward look and an inward look will have an outward expression of service unto the Lord. The psalmist encourages us to "serve the Lord with gladness" (Psalm 100:2).

Worship postures us to receive from God and to be useful for service. In worship, we become aware of the gravity of our need and His ability and willingness to meet it.

CHAPTER 5

Christ's Willingness

*"And behold, a leper came and worshiped Him,
saying, 'Lord, if You are willing, You can make me clean.'
Then Jesus put out His hand and touched him, saying,
'I am willing; be cleansed.'"*

MATTHEW 8:2-3

A little boy was eagerly looking forward to the birthday party of a friend who lived only a few blocks away. When the day finally arrived, a snow blizzard made the sidewalks and roads nearly impassable. The lad's father, sensing the danger, hesitated to let his son go.

The youngster reacted tearfully. "But Dad," he pleaded, "all the other kids will be there. Their parents are letting them go."

The father thought for a moment, then replied softly, "All right, you may go."

Surprised but overjoyed, the boy bundled up and plunged into the raging storm. The driving snow made visibility almost impossible, and it took him more than a half hour to trudge the short distance to the party.

As he rang the doorbell, he turned briefly to look out into the storm. His eye caught the shadow of a retreating figure. It was his father. He had followed his son's every step to make sure he arrived safely.

If a human father can display love like that to his son, how much more can our heavenly Father? God is a good Father. God is a giving Father. He loves to provide for His children. We read about this aspect of God in Luke 11:10-13.

> "Don't bargain with God. Be direct. Ask for what you need. This is not a cat-and-mouse, hide-and-seek game we're in. If your little boy asks for a serving of fish, do you scare him with a live snake on his plate? If your little girl asks for an egg, do you trick her with a spider? As bad as you are, you wouldn't think of such a thing—you're at least decent to your own children. And don't you think the Father who conceived you in love will give the Holy Spirit when you ask him?" (MSG).

The leper in Matthew 8 approached Jesus because of his great need to be free from his sickness. Many times we think we're the only ones having needs, but have you ever thought about God having needs? I know it seems like a crazy thought, but just think about it for a minute. Does God have needs that we can fulfill? We know that God doesn't need any material things, for He has it all. God doesn't need love, for He is Love. Then what does God need? In order to answer that question, we must know and understand the nature of God.

God's Nature

The nature of God is to give. The most well-known verse of the Bible tells us—"'For God so loved the world that He gave . . .'" (John 3:16). Jesus also taught that "'. . . it is more blessed to give than to receive'" (Acts 20:35). The Scripture goes on to say, "'The Son of Man came not to be ministered unto, but to minister'" (Matthew 20:28).

This latter verse seems to point to the self-sufficiency of God, which would lead us to believe that God doesn't need anything. Yet I believe He has a basic need. He who is Love and who is Good must express that love and goodness. He must give of His love and goodness—of His very Person. And that, I believe, is His need—to give!

This need to give is evident in the life of Christ. For example, in John 4, Jesus was at the well where the Samaritan woman came to draw water. Jesus started talking to her and asked her for a drink. She was surprised that He talked to her because Jews didn't talk to the Samaritans. Jesus said to her, "'If you knew the generosity of God and who I am, you would be asking *me* for a drink, and I would give you fresh, living water'" (John 4:10, MSG). He started the conversation with her because Jesus had a need; He needed water. But more importantly to the woman, He needed to give her what she was longing for.

The woman responded to Jesus and received the living water, and her life was changed. Giving to the woman satisfied His need. Someone has said, "It is not what God receives from us that satisfies Him, but what He can convince us to receive from Him that brings Him pleasure." When we understand the nature of God as a Giver, we understand that God's more than willing to meet us at the point of our need and satisfy us.

Types of Doubters

Many don't know the character of God; therefore, they doubt His willingness to meet them at their point of need. In the Scriptures, we find there are *two types of doubters*.

The first type are those who have no clue as to the ability of God. We have such a man in the story recorded in Mark 9:14-29. This man was a father who had a son that was demon–possessed. Upon hearing from people that he should take his son to Jesus and His disciples, he went without any knowledge about Jesus. One would think He at least thought Jesus could somehow help him or his son, but Jesus' ability to bring complete deliverance and healing to the child probably was unknown to him.

There are people all around us who are like this man; they have no revelation of God. We must always magnify the Person and power of Christ so that people may know who He is and call to Him.

The second type of doubter is like the leper who had full confidence in the power of God to heal, but he lacked the assurance of Jesus' willingness to heal. In both categories, it's amazing to think that people would doubt God's ability and willingness to heal.

The second type of doubter is like the leper who had full confidence in the power of God to heal, but he lacked the assurance of Jesus' willingness to heal.

Both types of people are common even today. Some individuals simply don't believe for themselves. They can pray for someone else and believe for him, but they just find it too difficult to believe for themselves. Other people have been wrongly taught that God doesn't heal today. Maybe some have asked God and not received; therefore, they doubt the promises and the power of God. Still others may be ignorant of the promises and truth of the Bible. It could be a number of things.

The leper knew Jesus as Lord, and that's why he worshiped Him. But he didn't know of His character when it came to His willingness to heal. Many times we can know one thing about God and in another area be completely unaware of who He really is. We need to spend time in God's Word. We have to allow the Holy Spirit to teach us so that we can grow in our knowledge of God.

We also need to have a proper image of God in all the areas of our lives. If a friend was going to doubt my relationship with him, I would much rather he doubted my ability to help than my willingness to do so. I would rather hear the words, "I'm sure you would help me if you could," rather than, "I know you can help me, but I'm not sure whether you will help me." Jesus answered the question not only for the leper in Matthew 8, but He answered for generations to come—Jesus is willing to cleanse anyone that comes to Him!

The Action of Believers

The leper isn't the first example of God's willingness to heal. The willingness of God to heal His people is recorded in the Scriptures right from the very beginning—from the book of Genesis!

We see in Genesis 20:17—"God healed Abimelech, his wife, and his female servants. Then they bore *children . . . .*"

The most striking passage of Scripture for healing is found in Exodus 15. The children of Israel were thirsty for water and could not find water. Finally, when they arrived at a place called Marah, they found water, but the water was bitter in taste. So the people complained to Moses. Moses prayed. God showed Moses a tree and told him to cast that tree in the water, and the waters were made sweet.

This was again the picture of the work of the cross. The tree wasn't the source of healing, but Moses' obedience and faith in the words of God brought the miracle. Moses obeyed, and the people enjoyed sweet waters.

There, in that place, God made a covenant with the children of Israel: "'If you diligently heed the voice of the LORD your God and do what is right in His sight, give ear to His commandments and keep all His statutes, I will put none of the diseases on you which I have brought on the Egyptians. For I *am* the LORD who heals you'" (Exodus 15:26). Here they received a revelation of the name of God which the Israelites hadn't known before, the name—*Jehovah Rapha*—the Lord who heals. The intimate title *Jehovah Rapha* reveals four principles.

We must diligently heed the voice of God. This first point means that we have to be led by the Spirit. You can keep all the other laws and, if the Spirit doesn't lead you, you may still lose your help and lose your healing. Hearing the Holy Spirit is a part of knowing the healing powers of *Jehovah Rapha*. We know that, even in prosperity, we can be doing all the right things, but if the Spirit doesn't lead us and we're in the "wrong place at the wrong time," we may not get our providential supply from God.

Healing operates in a similar way. The leading of the Holy Spirit and the Word of God work together. You can keep uttering

God's healing promises from His Word all the time, but if the Holy Spirit tells you to cut back on eating certain foods and you don't listen to Him, you can still be sick. If the Holy Spirit tells you not to nurse resentment and grudges against an individual, and you don't listen, you can still suffer bodily hurt and sickness. Many try to keep the letter of the Word without following the Spirit. The healing law may not work. Because God knows the causes of sicknesses and diseases, He tells the Israelite people to observe His laws.

We must do what is right in His sight. There are two words in this principle that provide insight—*do* and *right*. These two words can be more appropriately called *righteousness*. Righteousness and healing are Siamese twins; they go together. There's no point trying to get healed if you're living in sin. Now of course, the unbeliever can come for healing, as it is a demonstration of the mercy of God, so that salvation can be revealed to that person, but for the believer much more is expected.

> Please hear me. I'm not saying every sick person is sick because of personal sin. But I'm saying some are.

For the believer, we know the truth, and our sin must be cleansed as we approach God. A lot of people don't get healed because they still want to continue to live in sin. Remember that it's the original sin of Adam and Eve that brought sickness, disease, and death in the first place. Please hear me. I'm not saying every sick person is sick because of personal sin. But I'm saying some are. The principles outlined in James 5:13-16 clearly reveal to us that confession of sin and repentance may be necessary before the elders, or praying persons, actually pray for a brother or sister so that the prayer of faith is effective in bringing healing.

We must give ear to His commandments. The commandments refer to God's Word. In Proverbs 4, a father gives instructions to his son. He says, "My son, give attention to my words; incline your ear to my sayings. Do not let them depart from your eyes; keep them in the midst of your heart; for they *are* life to those who find them, and health to all their flesh" (vv. 20-22). One of the commandments is to love our neighbor. Many of us harbor unforgiveness and envy against our neighbor. I've seen those who actually didn't need prayer for healing, they just needed to forgive their brother, sister, friend, or neighbor. In other cases, I've seen those who have needed to start tithing again. Still others have needed to use their tongue to bless and encourage rather than curse and discourage. Simply doing God's commands has brought healing to their bodies.

The Bible says that, if we honor our father and mother, we will have long life and things will go well with us—"Honor your father and your mother, that your days may be long upon the land which the Lord your God is giving you" (Exodus 20:12). Ephesians reminds us to *"Honor your father and mother,'* which is the first commandment with promise . . ." (6:2). In this case, if we would simply obey God's instruction regarding honoring our parents, the Lord will maintain our health.

We must keep all His statutes. The fourth principle is following the pattern (statutes) of Scripture for healing from God. For example, when you are sick, the Bible says call the elders and let them anoint you with oil, and their prayer of faith shall heal you (James 5:14-15). When you follow the statute, the healing of *Jehovah Rapha* will be manifested. In your prayer, begin to hallow the name of *Jehovah Rapha* and follow the principles associated with the name.

God is willing to heal His people. You might say, "Well, that was in the Old Covenant. We're living in the New Covenant, and I don't think that applies to us, that covenant was with the children of Israel." If God healed people in the Old Covenant, how much more will He heal in the New Covenant, for the Bible says in Hebrews 7:22 and 8:6, that we have a "better covenant." Remember our God is a covenant-making, covenant-revealing, covenant-enabling, and covenant-keeping God.

Exodus not only records the healing covenant, but the revelation of the name of God, as *Rapha*—Healer. Since healer is one of

His names, it reveals one of His attributes of nature. What God is by nature, He never ceases to be, for the Scriptures also say, "'For I *am* the LORD, I do not change'" (Malachi 3:6).

Since healer is one of His names, it reveals one of His attributes of nature.

Jesus' answer to the leprous person answered the *if* question once and for all. When praying for your healing, don't pray, *"If* it be Your will," because the will of God is known clearly to us. When the will of God isn't known, then you can pray using *if.* But when the will of God is known, the *if* statement actually doubts God.

The Bible says in 1 John 5:14, when we pray or ask according to the will of God, He hears us. Amen. The willingness of God is displayed in His will, the Word of God. Jesus is willing to heal you. Every chance you get, tell others that Christ has the ability to heal and that He's willing to heal anyone who comes to Him and acknowledges Him as *Rapha.*

Repentance

Jesus, after fasting and praying for forty days, came out of the wilderness, and the first word He spoke was, "Repent!" In the Greek, repent or *metanoeo* means to turn around, to change our thinking, to get new thoughts, to think differently or to reconsider (Strong, "Greek Dictionary of the New Testament," 47). So repentance is a decision to change our intentions and ultimately our actions. It's what we need to do when we realize we have misunderstood God's Word and heart or haven't had the right or biblical mindset.

Time and again, I've discovered many are not receiving their healing because of things like misunderstanding, unbelief, and exposure to wrong teaching or influence. This is so sad to me. To think that these could receive if only they would realize their error and repent is disheartening indeed.

I've noticed those who have repented after they've been taught from the Scriptures. Understanding has come into their lives, and suddenly they're ready to receive from God. Others don't give time to soak in the Word of God and follow the aforementioned principles. These, it seems, give more time and respect to doctors than they do to God. If, for example, a doctor had given them certain instructions to follow for three months, the doctor's instructions would be obeyed. I wonder—if their pastors gave them a prescription from the Word of God, would they lose patience and neglect the instruction? If we would only give the same opportunity to the Word of God and the principles of exercising our faith in it as we do to the doctors and their prescriptions, I'm convinced we would see real results!

Hebrews 11:6 tells us, "But without faith *it is* impossible to please Him, for he who comes to God must believe that He is, and that He is a rewarder of those who diligently seek Him." Our responsibility is to exercise our faith in the One who is willing and able to heal us, believing He'll grant our requests and petitions as His Word promises us He'll do. Then, we can receive healing just like the leper did, leaving Christ's presence and testifying of the gracious gift He's given to us.

CHAPTER 6

Testify & Keep Your Healing!

*"And Jesus said to him, 'See that you tell no one;
but go your way, show yourself to the priest, and offer the gift
that Moses commanded, as a testimony to them.'"*

MATTHEW 8:4

Charles Wesley wrote his first hymn just three days after his conversion. That hymn was "O for a Thousand Tongues to Sing." What a testimony to his salvation! Over the years, he is said to have written 6,500 hymns and gospel songs of every conceivable subject.

Like Wesley, a man who has allowed the Word of God to dwell richly in his life is a man who is quick and ready to praise and testify about God. When we testify about what God's done in our lives, we seal His blessing. John, the writer of Revelation, affirms this fact when he wrote:

> Then I heard a loud voice saying in heaven, "Now salvation, and strength, and the kingdom of our God, and the power of His Christ have come, for the accuser of our brethren, who accused them before our God day and night, has been cast down. And they overcame him by the blood of the Lamb and by the word of their testimony, and they did not love their lives to the death" (Revelation 12:10-11).

As we have been considering the healing of the leper, we have come to the point in the story where Jesus instructs him to go see the priest and offer the gift that Moses commanded as a testimony to the priest. This verse speaks volumes to us, so let's examine it point by point.

"Tell No One"

I want to suggest three possible reasons for Jesus telling the leper to tell no one. First, Jesus may have wanted this man and others to fulfill the Law and offer the testimony that Moses commanded.

The Jewish rabbis taught that cleansing lepers should be a characteristic of the Messiah. In those times, no doctor or person could heal leprosy. The priest knew only God could heal a leper. It was a testimony to the priest that Messiah had come.

The second possible reason may have been Jesus set an example of putting healings to the test. Any person maintaining she's healed when she's not isn't only deceived but unscriptural. We should never reject the idea of verification by a medical expert. What God does supernaturally can be verified in the natural realm.

The third possible reason may have been Jesus wanted the man's healing to be protected from naysayers and mockers. There are times people receive healing, but people around them begin to mock and discredit the healing. The atmosphere of faith, expectancy, blessing, and healing isn't only necessary to receive from God, but it's also necessary to maintain the blessing of the Lord.

At times, Jesus took people away from this kind of atmosphere. Once He took a man outside the city to heal him. Another time, when He entered a house to raise a dead girl, He told everyone to be out of the room. It's so important not only for healing, but for everything that we receive from the Lord—that we maintain it.

Another way to maintain a healing is to keep a faith-filled atmosphere. We must acknowledge there are times we need to remove ourselves or others from an atmosphere of unbelief, mockery, or skepticism so that we or others may both receive and maintain healing.

"Show Yourself . . . Offer the Gift"

Once the leper, who was then healed, came to see the priest, the priest was required to offer a gift or a sacrifice on his behalf. As we noticed in our discussion in a previous chapter, certain cases of cleansing required the recipient to make an offering to the Lord. In the leper's case, the priest had to give the sacrifice. What a true picture of healing this is! It's God the Father giving His Son as a sacrifice for our healing.

The priest then would come and examine the leper to verify the healing; he would bring two live birds, cedar wood, scarlet, and hyssop for the sacrifice. One bird was to be killed in an earthen vessel over running water (Leviticus 14:5). The priest would then take the living bird and dip it in the blood of the dead bird, then sprinkle it seven times on the cleansed leper, pronouncing the leper clean and releasing the living bird to go free in an open field (vv. 6-7).

After he did this, the priest was to take two lambs and offer them also as a sacrifice and then take the blood of the lamb and anoint the tip of the right ear, the thumb of the right hand, and the great toe of the right foot of the leper (v. 14). Once the blood was applied, the priest would take oil and anoint the right ear, right thumb, and right great toe of the man, where the blood was applied (v. 17).

The reason for highlighting this law mentioned in Leviticus is that those principles apply to us today. Once people receive healing, they also need to be taught to maintain the healing. One of the first things we have to learn is to testify with our mouths what God has done for us.

I've known people who were wonderfully healed by God, but after some time they lost their healing. I believe and teach that this happens at times because those healed have failed to give God glory and instead given access to the Devil in their lives. Not only that, just as the leper was commanded to go to the temple and see the priest, we have to learn to be part of a fellowship—a local church—where we and others can give witness to God's gracious work in our lives. We all need to be a part of a local church where we're nourished and strengthened by God's Word and fellowship with believers.

As a pastor, it's amazing to see how many people leave the church and stop fellowshiping with believers once they have received what they need. But it's never surprised me that, after some time, they lost what God gave them.

Looking back at the laws regarding the cleansing of lepers, we see they had to be anointed with the blood and the oil. The Bible says in 2 Corinthians 7:1, "Therefore, having these promises, beloved, let us cleanse ourselves from all filthiness of the flesh and spirit, perfecting holiness in the fear of God." If we're to keep the blessing of God in our lives, then we need to have a daily spiritual bath by the blood of Jesus and the anointing of the Holy Spirit.

If we're to keep the blessing of God in our lives, then we need to have a daily spiritual bath by the blood of Jesus and the anointing of the Holy Spirit.

The blood and the oil being applied to their ear, hand, and foot represents a believer who is able to hear God, do what's right, and walk in righteousness. It's the requirement of the covenant of Exodus 15:26 to "'diligently heed the voice of the Lord . . . and do what is right in His sight, give ear to His commandments and keep all His statutes.'"

John 5 records an instance when Jesus saw a man who was lying on his bed for years and told him, "'Rise, take up your bed and walk'" (v. 5). This man was immediately healed. After his healing, one day, as Jesus came to the temple, He saw him again and said to him, "'Sin no more, lest a worse thing come upon you.'" Here Jesus warned the man who He had healed to stop sinning in order to keep what he had received and avoid something worse coming upon his life.

Jesus spoke specifically of something like this happening in Matthew 12:43-45—

"When an unclean spirit goes out of a man, he goes through dry places, seeking rest, and finds none. Then he says, 'I will return to my house from which I came.' And when he comes, he finds *it* empty, swept, and put in order. Then he goes and takes with him seven other spirits more wicked than himself, and they enter and dwell there; and the last *state* of that man is worse than the first. So shall it also be with this wicked generation."

Many times a person is healed not by her faith, but by the faith of others, so she has to learn to develop herself in God's Word and shun all the attacks of the enemy. Her faith, confession, and attitude have to be developed by the Word of God.

I know numerous examples of people who came to a service and hands were laid on them with prayer and they received their healing. Yet a few weeks later, the symptoms and sickness came back upon them. Why? I believe we don't emphasize enough how to maintain our healing. When Jesus speaks of the unclean spirit seeking rest, He literally says the unclean spirit will go back to the person it left, and finding him clean, he'll go and get seven more unclean spirits that are more wicked than he to dwell in the man. That's the Devil's strategy—to torment, harass, and bring back the uncleanness or sickness. Therefore, we have to learn to grow in the Word of God, and let it be a shield round about us, protecting us from the oppression of the enemy.

When you are healed, testify of your healing; it puts your life in the place of submission to God, acknowledging that God is your Healer. Remember to fellowship with those who build your faith and walk in righteousness. You, too, continue to walk in obedience to God's Word and commands so that you can keep what God has given you. Testify and keep your healing!

As we continue on our journey, let's look at the relationship between faith and healing. Remember, the Holy Spirit is alongside to help bring understanding to our hearts.

PART II

The Faith Factor

CHAPTER 7

Favor or Faith?

*"So Jesus answered and said to them,
'If you can believe, all things are possible to him who believes.'"*

MARK 9:23

I read a story once about an old sailor who repeatedly got lost at sea. His friends gave him a compass and urged him to use it. The next time he went out in his boat, he followed their advice and took the compass with him. But as usual he became hopelessly confused and was unable to find land. Finally he was rescued by his friends. Disgusted and impatient with him, they asked, "Why didn't you use that compass we gave you? You could have saved us a lot of trouble!"

The sailor responded, "I didn't dare to! I wanted to go north, but as hard as I tried to make the needle aim in that direction, it just kept on pointing southeast."

The old sailor was so certain he knew which was north that he stubbornly tried to force his own personal persuasion onto his compass. Unable to do so, he tossed it aside as worthless and failed to benefit from the guidance it offered (*10,000 Sermon* "Guidance").

Like the old sailor, we approach God's Word to find things that *validate* our system of belief rather than going to God's Word to *generate* our system of belief. When it comes to healing, I've known people who've decided what they want to believe and how their healing should happen. Then they go to the Word of God and try to find Scriptures and stories that will validate their theories.

When we approach God's Word, we need to approach it with a humble attitude and a teachable heart. We need to believe—to exercise our faith—for God's healing.

When we talk about healing, the issue of faith always arises. I've heard people say something like this to those in need of healing: "The reason you're in the hospital bed is because you don't have faith." I've had friends who lived in such torment and guilt because some men of God told them they didn't have faith for their healing.

> I've had friends who lived in such torment and guilt because some men of God told them they didn't have faith for their healing.

When I hear things like this, I wonder why men of God would want to say such discouraging things. I would think they would want to speak things that would build an individual's faith instead of condemning him or her. We don't need condemnation; what we need is faith for healing!

I've needed a breakthrough in my life on a few occasions. I've had moments where I've been acutely aware of not having the faith I've needed for healing. What I've needed at those times is someone to tell me how to receive faith to support my pursuit for healing. I've definitely not needed someone seemingly placing blame on me, the sick one, for my not possessing the healing I've needed.

At those times, my actual need was for someone to minister life and faith to me. The Word of God says in Romans 10:17, "Faith *comes* by hearing." And in my frailty I've needed someone to remind me of the biblical accounts of healings, someone to testify to me of personal healings, thus creating an atmosphere where I could receive from God.

In this part of the book, we're going to examine Scripture to see if faith is always required or if God performs healings without faith. My friend, Bubba Grimsley, always says, "Whenever two or three people gather in the name of Jesus, Jesus shows up, and when Jesus shows up, He loves to show off."

I believe Bubba's right. Many times, God comes and does exactly what He wants to do, when He wants to do it. And we know

He can do it to whomsoever He wills just because He's God. Here's a story that highlights this.

An Unexpected Healing

A wealthy and well-to-do businessman by the name of Richard was attending a special meeting organized by churches of a certain city. He had a chauffeur named Todd who drove him everywhere. Usually Todd drove Richard to any place he wanted to go and then parked the car and waited in the car.

So on this particular day, the meeting was being held on a big open field. There was at least 30,000 people in that field. Per his usual, Richard was dropped off by his chauffeur, and his chauffeur went to one side of the field, parked the car, and waited until the meeting was over.

As the worship music time ended, suddenly the evangelist, who was the speaker for that night, went to the platform and began to lead people in a prayer time before preaching from the Word of God. As soon as he finished praying, he said, "I see in a vision, that there is a man, you have problems with your liver. You also have a skin disorder. You're here, and you're sitting on top of a black car. Jesus is healing you right now."

Todd was sitting on the hood of the car, minding his own business, reading a newspaper, and just casually giving a little attention to what was happening. As soon as the evangelist said those words, immediately, Todd's skin condition was healed, and Todd was shocked. His entire attention went immediately to the evangelist on the platform. After some time, the evangelist called people who were healed to come forward.

Todd went to Richard and told him what he just had experienced. He even asked Richard if he could go to the stage and give his testimony. Up until this time, Todd had never been in a meeting like this. On Sundays, he used to drop off Richard at church, but he always declined the offer to come inside. He had no clue as to what really happened in meetings like these. But on this occasion, Jesus had touched his life.

Richard allowed Todd to go share his experience, and as soon as he came on stage, the evangelist began to ask him, "Have you given your heart to Jesus?"

"No!" said Todd.

"Did you come here for a healing or touch from Jesus?" the evangelist continued to question him.

"No," Todd answered.

A little taken back by Todd's two negative responses to his questions, he then asked him, "Why then did you come tonight?"

"I'm a chauffeur for a company, and my boss is here in the audience. I drove him here and was waiting in the very back, leaning on the hood of the car, and suddenly, I saw my skin being healed."

Praise God! This man was clueless about everything going on in that service, not even paying any attention to it, when God met Him.

I personally witnessed this account. It caused me to reflect on the sovereignty of God. I became more aware of the fact that God can do exactly what He wants to do, exactly when He wants to do it, and to whomsoever He wills. I've heard people teach that, without faith, it is impossible for someone to receive healing. But in this story, we see that Todd didn't come looking for healing. He was an unbeliever who had never responded to, much less heard, the gospel of Jesus Christ, yet Jesus reached out to him. That night he not only gave his testimony of healing, but he made Jesus the Lord of his life.

Two Factors

As I study the Scriptures in regard to healing, I've discovered two factors related to healings and miracles. I call them the *favor factor* and the *tango factor*.

Favor factor is a term I use to refer to a class of healings and miracles that are performed without the apparent cooperation or activation of another person's faith. In this class, God heals and performs as He wills, when He wills, and to whomever He wills. I've used the term *favor* because it means receiving something we really didn't do anything to deserve. Of course, this has to do with the sovereignty of God. As God said to Moses in Exodus 33:19, "'. . . I will be gracious to whom I will be gracious, and I will have compassion on whom I will have compassion.'" He's sovereign, and He can do what He wants.

We have many examples in the Scripture that attest to the favor factor—examples of people who received from God without ever having faith or expectancy. Luke gives us a great example. Let's read it from the seventh chapter.

> Now it happened, the day after, *that* He went into a city called Nain; and many of His disciples went with Him, and a large crowd. And when He came near the gate of the city, behold, a dead man was being carried out, the only son of his mother; and she was a widow. And a large crowd from the city was with her. When the Lord saw her, He had compassion on her and said to her, "Do not weep." Then He came and touched the open coffin, and those who carried *him* stood still. And He said, "Young man, I say to you, arise." So he who was dead sat up and began to speak. And He presented him to his mother. Then fear came upon all, and they glorified God, saying, "A great prophet has risen up among us"; and, "God has visited His people" (vv. 11-16).

Again, we find that there was no faith exercised on the part of the woman who lost her son or on the part of any close relative. Jesus simply saw the woman weeping and had compassion on her. Right away, He cancelled the funeral by bringing miraculous healing to the family in the raising of this widow's son.

There are numerous biblical accounts that display the compassion of Jesus for the lives of people. It's God's will that every person knows He's good. God's desire is that every person comes to know Him and see His wonderful works. So when we see God working in the lives of humans, even when they don't have faith or haven't exercised any trust in Him, it displays His mercy, compassion, and love.

In Luke 5, we find Simon Peter back from an unsuccessful fishing trip. Jesus showed up, gave him an instruction or two, and miraculously provided a huge haul of fish. Simon didn't have any faith at all. He simply obeyed Jesus' instructions. Many healings and miracles would come to us if we simply obeyed the instruction given us, even if we didn't have faith for them ourselves.

Many healings and miracles would come to us if we simply obeyed the instruction given us, even if we didn't have faith for them ourselves.

Twice Jesus fed a crowd with little food and the power of miracles—once a crowd of 5,000 and another time a crowd of 4,000. Through the obedient actions of a few individuals, Jesus worked miracles in feeding so many. We've probably sung the song, "Trust and Obey." It's true. We need to trust and obey God. Even when we struggle with trusting Him, it would do us well to obey Him still, knowing that He's able and willing to bring about breakthroughs in our lives.

The second dynamic that we see in the Scriptures when it comes to a person's receiving anything from God is what I call the *tango factor*. We hear the common line, "It takes two to tango." That's where I get this term because certain healings and miracles require both divine action *and* human cooperation. The divine action required is *anointing*. And the necessary human cooperation is *faith*.

When studying the healing ministry of Jesus, a *majority* of the time we see the tango factor, where Jesus required faith from the sick person wanting healing or from the nearest relative or friend of the person.

In Luke 4, Jesus was in the synagogue, and He preached a powerful prophetic sermon, but the people didn't respond correctly. We read:

So all bore witness to Him, and marveled at the gracious words which proceeded out of His mouth. And they said, "Is this not Joseph's son?" He said to them, "You will surely say this proverb to Me, 'Physician, heal yourself! Whatever we have heard done in Capernaum, do also here in Your country.'" Then He said, "Assuredly, I say to you, no prophet is accepted in his own country. But I tell you truly, many widows were in Israel in the days of Elijah, when the heaven was shut up three years and six months, and there was a great famine throughout all the land; but to none of them was Elijah sent except to Zarephath, *in the region* of Sidon, to a woman *who was* a widow. And many lepers were in Israel in the time of Elisha the prophet, and none of them was cleansed except Naaman the Syrian" (vv. 22-27).

Often, when people read Jesus' words in verse 23, they ask, "How can Jesus heal Himself?" Actually, the phrase, "Physician, heal thyself," could be best translated, "Physician, heal and do it yourself."

What the people were saying was, "Perform for us! We don't want to participate in your activities. We know your father, mother, and family, and you're the boy next door. Suddenly, you're doing all these miracles everywhere else, so show us some stuff." They wanted Jesus to perform without having any intention of cooperating with Him.

Jesus answered them by comparing them to two events which happened in the Old Testament in the times of Elijah and Elisha. Jesus said the people from His hometown were no different from the people in the time of Elijah. Then a great sign was performed for people to turn to God; instead, the people of Elijah's day moaned and complained. No one was willing to exercise faith and obey God.

Elijah prayed for the rain to cease, and it ceased for three years. You would have thought they would call out to God for rain, trusting the same God who stopped it could cause it to rain again. No one was willing to work with God save the woman at Zarephath. God sent Elijah to this woman who was willing to exercise her faith to see breakthrough.

The other event Jesus referred to in Luke 4 was when Naaman went to see Elisha in 2 Kings 5. Naaman was a gentile whose wife had a young girl from the land of Israel as her servant. The servant girl believed that, if Naaman were with the prophet Elisha, he would be made well. We know that initially Naaman didn't want to do what Elisha instructed him to do, but eventually he was willing to obey and exercise his faith.

Highlighting these two events in Luke 4, Jesus was saying that people in His day were no different than those in Elijah's and Elisha's days. He was basically telling them, "I'm in my hometown, but no one is willing to exercise faith. No one is willing to put a demand on the anointing." He was saying, "I'm not moved by crowds, but by faith. I will pass thousands of people just to find one person who is willing to exercise faith and obey."

All the people from His hometown had to do was draw on the anointing that was present and Jesus would heal the sick and deliver the oppressed.

You see, Jesus had just finished preaching a powerful sermon proclaiming: *"'The Spirit of the Lord is upon Me, because He has anointed Me to preach the gospel to the poor; He has sent Me to heal the brokenhearted, to proclaim liberty to the captives and recovery of sight to the blind, to set at liberty those who are oppressed; to proclaim the acceptable year of the Lord'"* (Luke 4:18-19). All the people from His hometown had to do was draw on the anointing that was present and Jesus would heal the sick and deliver the oppressed.

Over and over again, today, people come to church with this attitude towards the minister. It's like they're saying, "I'm waiting for you to perform. I'm waiting for you to minister to me, and I will sit here until you do something." These people may even come in sick, but sadly, they'll go home that way if they continue to not exercise their own faith.

If, however, the same people came with the attitude of faith to receive from God and obey and respect the anointing on the minister, they would receive from Him. God never has rebuked faith. Twice, in the Bible, Jesus commended individuals for having "great faith." The sad thing is that on both occasions the persons were not Israelites. The ones He commended for their faith were actually people who had no covenant with God. If a person who has no covenant with God can approach Jesus with "great faith," how much more we, who have a better covenant—ratified by the blood of Jesus—need to approach God with faith that we'll receive from Him.

As we've been talking about the leper who stepped out of the crowd in the previous chapters, it's interesting to me that, when he got healed, no one else stepped out to receive from Jesus. I find it almost unbelievable that more people didn't ask for healing once they saw the anointing of Jesus heal the leper. But the fact is that often people don't want to exercise faith to receive from God. I've met a lot of people who are sick, but they really don't want to exercise faith in God. They'll exercise faith in the doctor and obey the doctor who tells them to take medication three times a day for twenty-one days. They'll even believe that they will be made well by their following the doctor's instructions.

> **If a person who has no covenant with God can approach Jesus with "great faith," how much more we, who have a better covenant—ratified by the blood of Jesus— need to approach God with faith that we'll receive from Him.**

However, Hebrews 11:6 tells us, "But without faith it is impossible to please and be satisfactory to Him. For whoever would come near to God must [necessarily] believe that God exists and that He is the rewarder of those who earnestly and diligently seek Him [out]" (AMP). The very act of a person approaching God is an act of faith. This verse does not say for us to sit down and wait for God to come to us. No! It affirms that, if we want to come close to Him, we first must believe He is God and then believe He is a "rewarder."

James 4:8 encourages us to "draw near to God and He will draw near to" us. We have to learn to exercise our faith to believe that God exists and God wants to reward us. Furthermore, we ought to embrace the promise given in James—that God will meet us when we approach Him. Looking at Ephesians 3:20, we see additional evidence of God's desire for us in that it says He "is able to [carry out His purpose and] do superabundantly, far over *and* above all that we [dare] ask or think [infinitely beyond our highest prayers, desires, thoughts, hopes, or dreams]" (AMP).

Some people think that we need to have some giant faith to receive anything from God. This isn't supported by the sermon Jesus preached on the mustard seed. Jesus said faith the size of a mustard seed would move a mountain (Luke 17:6). There are those individuals today who have studied faith to the point it should be mountain-size in their lives, but they can't even move a mustard seed with their faith. It's not the size of our faith that's important; it's our willingness to put faith to work, to actually exercise it toward what we need.

But we must remember also, that our God is gracious. He shines His favor upon those He would, healing them whether they have faith or not.

CHAPTER 8

Got Faith?

*"Jesus answered said to him, 'If you can believe,
all things are possible to him who believes.'"*

MARK 9:23

I believe we see four basic types of people in Scripture and in life. Second Thessalonians 3:2 mentions that "not everyone has faith." There are *unbelievers,* our first type of people, and they *have no faith in God.*

Then, there are those *unbelievers* who *don't know God but have heard people testify of His character, His power, and His willingness to heal.* The scribe in Mark 12:28-34 might be considered an example of this type of unbeliever.

The third people type is *born again by the blood of Jesus, is discipled by Christ, and is studying the Scriptures, walking in the faith.* As 2 Corinthians 5:7 says, such individuals "walk by faith"; they regulate their lives and conduct themselves by their "conviction or belief respecting man's relationship to God and divine things, with trust and holy fervor" (AMP). They, then, walk by faith and not by sight.

The last people type is what I like to call *unbelieving believers.* These are *people who have faith in God for salvation and maybe other things but don't have faith in the area of their need.* They're full of unbelief in that area. These are people who have no active faith for certain issues or needs in their lives. They may even believe that God can and has done things in the past. They believe that God can and will do things in the future, but their faith isn't active for their present need.

These, too, may have faith in one area of their lives but not in another area. For example, I know people who have faith when it comes to their finances. When they're in need of miraculous provision, they can believe God, stand on the promises of God, and see financial breakthrough. The same people, however, may not have faith for God to heal them of an inconvenient headache.

I want to deal with the fourth category of people because that's where most of us are. To a certain degree, all believers have faith. Our problem, however, is having faith in the area of our need. The story of Mary, Martha, and Lazarus is a great example of this.

No Faith for Resurrection

Jesus decided to visit Bethany where Mary, Martha, and Lazarus made their home. Before His coming, Lazarus had been sick for awhile, and the sisters had sent news for Jesus to come to Bethany. But Jesus delayed and said, "'This sickness is not unto death, but for the glory of God, that the Son of God may be glorified through it'" (John 11:4).

After some days, Lazarus died. So this was the reason for His visit to Bethany, not to attend a funeral but to display the glory of God. For He told his disciples in John 11:11, "'Our friend Lazarus sleeps, but I go that I may wake him up.'"

As soon as Martha knew that Jesus had come, she ran to Jesus and said, "'Lord, if You had been here, my brother would not have died'" (v. 21). You see, she had faith in Jesus to heal, but He had come too late, and now Lazarus was dead. Mary felt similarly, wishing He had come sooner. Both had faith in the anointing of Jesus to heal, but their faith was only going to manifest healing if Jesus had shown up before the death of Lazarus. Both had no real faith to believe that Jesus could do a miracle *now*!

When we look at the text, we find Jesus said to Martha, "'Your brother will rise again'" (v. 23).

"'I know he will rise again in the resurrection at the last day'" (v. 24), she responded, demonstrating by these words that she had faith in the promises of God for the future but no faith for the present need.

Jesus kept speaking words to her that would build her faith, but she couldn't see and recognize the anointing presently upon Jesus. Jesus told here, "'I am the resurrection and the life'" (v. 25).

Both the sisters were full of unbelief for the present. They believed Jesus could have raised up Lazarus when he was still alive and sick. It was quite another thing for them to believe Jesus could raise Lazarus from the dead. It's the same for many of us. We may think God could have done something for us back at one point, but now it's too late. We may even think it's one thing for God to work healing in a certain area of our lives, but another area seems unreachable.

As Jesus approached the tomb where Lazarus lay, the Scriptures record that Jesus wept (John 11:35). This is the shortest verse in the Bible. The Jews surrounding Jesus mistook His tears for sorrow that His friend was dead. I don't think Jesus was weeping because Lazarus was dead, but the whole purpose of Jesus coming to Bethany this time around was to raise Lazarus from the dead as He had told the disciples. I want to suggest the reason Jesus wept was due to the fact his dear friends didn't believe He could do anything for them now. Remember, He spent so much time with Martha, Mary, and Lazarus in Bethany. He was a frequent guest in their home. They should have had strong faith by now, yet in their hour of need, they had no active faith to trust Him. I believe it was the unbelief in Mary and Martha that made Jesus weep.

Unbelief will make Jesus weep. But the opposite is true also. Faith will make Jesus rejoice.

Unbelief will make Jesus weep. But the opposite is true also. Faith will make Jesus rejoice. I wanted to highlight this story to point out that Mary and Martha had faith in Jesus for other things but no faith at all for Lazarus's resurrection at that moment. In spite of their unbelief, Jesus performed a miracle. Again, here we see God performing the *favor fac-*

tor, where no human cooperation was involved. Our focus, on this part of the teaching, is on the *tango factor,* however, where faith is required on our side—where we need to learn to appropriate our faith to receive from God.

There are many like Martha and Mary in this story—those who don't appropriate faith to receive from God. They've heard that Jesus has done many mighty miracles and healings or have experienced some of these in their pasts, but they don't have active faith for the present, for *now!* There are people who, according to Hebrews 4:2, receive the promises but don't appropriate faith to receive the benefits. Though unaware of their own decision, people do choose to walk in unbelief.

Unbelief

Unbelief hinders the flow of miracles and healings. The Bible says in Mark 6:5-6, "Now He could do no mighty work there, except that He laid His hands on a few sick people and healed *them.* And He marveled because of their unbelief." This passage doesn't say that Jesus *wouldn't* heal, but that He *couldn't.*

It's rare to see healings and miracles in the atmosphere of strife, argument, division, fear, or unbelief unless the favor factor is operating—except where God comes and heals and works miracles in spite of the negative atmosphere. In Matthew 17, Jesus gives the disciples the reason for not seeing healing manifest in the child brought to them—"So Jesus said to them, 'Because of your unbelief; for assuredly, I say to you, if you have faith as a mustard seed, you will say to this mountain, "Move from here to there," and it will move; and nothing will be impossible for you'" (Matthew 17:20).

Let's look at another healing story in the life of Jesus in Mark 8:22-26.

> Then He came to Bethsaida; and they brought a blind man
> to Him, and begged Him to touch him. So He took the blind
> man by the hand and led him out of the town. And when He

had spit on his eyes and put His hands on him, He asked him if he saw anything. And he looked up and said, "I see men like trees, walking." Then He put *His* hands on his eyes again and made him look up. And he was restored and saw everyone clearly. Then He sent him away to his house, saying, "Neither go into the town, nor tell anyone in the town."

Here, some interesting questions arise. Why did Jesus take this man outside the city and heal him? Why did Jesus use spit? And why did He have to pray for him twice?

Well, the answer to the first question is quite simple. We find that the city Jesus took this blind man out of was the city of Bethsaida, and it was one of the three cities that Jesus rebuked for their unbelief. We read about this in Matthew 11:20-23.

Then He began to rebuke the cities in which most of His mighty works had been done, because they did not repent: "Woe to you, Chorazin! Woe to you, Bethsaida! For if the mighty works which were done in you had been done in Tyre and Sidon, they would have repented long ago in sackcloth and ashes. But I say to you, it will be more toler-able for Tyre and Sidon in the day of judgment than for you. And you, Capernaum, who are exalted to heaven, will be brought down to Hades; for if the mighty works which were done in you had been done in Sodom, it would have remained until this day."

Wow! I don't think much needs to be said after reading those verses. In each of the three cities, great miracles and healings were demonstrated, yet people failed to believe and receive Messiah. You might say that Jesus is God and He could heal in any atmosphere. I agree, but the man couldn't stay healed with all that unbelief sur-rounding him, so Jesus took him out of the city and also told him to not go back into that atmosphere.

This brings us to our second question, why did Jesus spit on this man's eyes? This seems really awkward. I've traveled all around the world, and I've never heard or known any culture or nation in which spitting is honorable. In every culture that I've known, spitting upon a person is always an insult. Even in the Scriptures, we have examples where spitting was considered an insult, including the time Jesus was spat upon—"Then they spat on Him, and took the reed and struck Him on the head" (Matthew 27:30). I've heard preachers preach this miracle story and say that Jesus' spit was different. It was a spit of power. It was a creative spit. Some have even gone on to explain all the science connected to it and why Jesus did it. I think many have missed the point. The point is that spitting is an insult, and when Jesus spat,

Jesus was insulting sickness and disease in the physical body.

He did not spit on the man but on the blindness. Jesus was insulting sickness and disease in the physical body.

We have two other instances when Jesus used His spit. Once in John 9:1-7, He took His spit and mud and put it on the eyes of the blind man. In the other instance, Jesus put spit on the tongue of a man with a speech impediment. In all these cases, Jesus applied spit on the place of the sickness. So in comparison with laying on of hands, we could say that Jesus laid hands on people, but put spit on the sickness or the works of the Devil. Even in this story, He put the spit on the blindness but laid hands on the person.

The third question that needs answering is, why did Jesus pray twice? I think this answer will help us with the issue of faith. When Jesus put spit and laid hands on the blind man, his eyes opened up, but still he couldn't see clearly. Jesus again laid His hands on him and asked him if he saw clearly. This time the man saw clearly. The second touch wasn't to release more power to the man. The man was more open to receive; he could at least see in part according to the measure of faith he had received. As he began to see progress, his faith increased, and so Jesus laid hands on him again, encouraging his faith.

You see, this man came from an atmosphere full of unbelief, and his faith was being developed right there in that moment. The issue isn't a matter of how many times to get prayer. The issue is that God's power is present, and we need to do whatever is necessary to receive full benefits of that. If you're sick and you go for prayer when your pastor calls and you don't get healed, that doesn't mean God doesn't want to heal you or that you don't have faith. Keep going every time there is a call for prayer and keep standing on the Word of God. Let each time build and increase your faith until the manifestation comes forth.

Every time you respond to a call like that, I believe God is doing something. You might not see it, but I believe every time God meets with us something is always deposited. I believe every time God does something in us it increases our faith. This man, when Jesus touched him the first time, received a start to his healing. Although it wasn't clear, it built a measure of faith to see the full manifestation of healing, so Jesus touched him again.

The Process

Faith is a process. When we hold a series of meetings at our church, I encourage people to come to the altar every time there is prayer for healing, and I've seen some people get healed the first night. Others have sat under the teaching of God's Word for a few days, and it's produced faith in them, and then they've received their healing.

Always remember that Bible faith begins in your spirit. Faith is an attribute activated by the Holy Spirit through the Word of God and, therefore, must be birthed by a spiritual process. When we hear God's Word preached or hear testimonies of His work, a seed faith is deposited in our spirits. Once faith in our spirits is activated, it moves to our soul realm.

The soul is made up of our mind, will, emotion, memory, and imaginations. Here, faith is processed. Faith helps the mind to line up with the promises of God. Faith can then be felt in our emotions. The memory recalls all the testimonies of great things about God and what He's done, and the imagination helps play a faith movie that builds hope. Finally, the will moves out in obedience to our faith, causing us to make decisions and take actions in line with our faith.

> The memory recalls all the testimonies of great things about God and what He's done, and the imagination helps play a faith movie that builds hope.

From the soul realm, faith moves to our bodies. Our bodies begin to move in response to our faith. Your body will display the action of faith, whether it's opening your mouth in faith-filled speech or physically getting up and walking towards a person with the anointing, or doing some kind of act of faith. This action is illustrated by the woman with the issue of blood approaching Jesus. Remember, she said, "'If only I may touch His clothes, I shall be made well'" (Mark 5:28). Faith caused her take physical action.

Blind Bartimaeus also put action to his faith by using his mouth, for it says in Mark 10:47, "And when he heard that it was Jesus of Nazareth, he began to cry out and say, 'Jesus, Son of David, have mercy on me!'"

William Booth in his message to the soldiers made this statement, "Faith and works should travel side by side, step answering to step, like the legs of men walking. First faith, and then works; and then faith again, and then works again—until they can scarcely distinguish which is the one and which is the other" (48). Or as the book of James 2:17 says, "Isn't it obvious that God-talk without God-acts is outrageous nonsense?" (MSG).

All of this reminds me of a story appropriate to the topic at hand.

A man fell off a cliff but managed to grab a tree limb on the way down. The following conversation ensued:

"Is anyone up there?"

"I am here. I am the Lord. Do you believe me?"

"Yes, Lord, I believe. I really believe, but I can't hang on much longer."

"That's all right, if you really believe you have nothing to worry about. I will save you. Just let go of the branch."

A moment of pause, then: "Is anyone else up there?" (*Bits & Pieces*, 3).

Isn't that just how we are? We want help, we want healing, and we want deliverance, but please don't make us work our faith for it. It's just too scary!

Maybe it would be helpful to see faith as a muscle that grows during times of stretching. When it takes times for a word to come to fulfillment, it's discouraging; nevertheless, we need to understand that faith is a process. And if we endure and don't lose hope, what we've asked for will surely come to pass.

Exercising Faith

I'm reminded also of Abraham's life of faith. God visited Abraham when he was 86 years old, but he didn't see the fulfillment of those promises made by God during the visitation until he was 100 years of age. For fourteen years, he stood on the promise of God allowing his faith to be developed and staying steady.

In Romans 4:20-21, we see four keys in the life of Abraham that will help us. It reads as follows: "He did not waver at the promise of God through unbelief, but was strengthened in faith, giving glory to God, and being fully convinced that what He had promised He was also able to perform."

The first key in Abraham's life of faith is that he didn't waver through unbelief. To waver here means to make use of one's own judgment and reasoning in discerning things. To stagger at the promise is to take into consideration the difficulties that lie ahead. We don't look to what lies ahead; we look to Jesus, the Author and Finisher of our faith. As long as Peter looked at Jesus while he was walking on water, his faith stabilized him. As soon as he took his eyes off Jesus and focused on the water, unbelief grew, and he began to sink. We have to look at the God of the promises.

The apostle Paul encourages us in 2 Corinthians 4:18 to ". . . not look at the things which are seen, but at the things which are not seen. For the things which are seen *are* temporary, but the things which are not seen *are* eternal."

When you are facing sickness in your body, then the thing that isn't seen is health and healing. The thing that is seen is the symptom. We don't deny that there is sickness in the body. We know there is sickness in the body, but we choose to focus our eyes, mouth, and everything on the unseen which is health. Philippians 4:8 says, "Finally, brethren, whatever things are true, whatever things *are* noble, whatever things *are* just, whatever things *are* pure, whatever things *are* lovely, whatever things *are* of good report, if *there is* any virtue and if *there is* anything praiseworthy—meditate on these things."

The second key in the life of Abraham is that he was strengthened in his faith. He did things that added to his faith. Second Peter 1:5-8 tells us to add to our faith "virtue, to virtue knowledge, to knowledge self-control, to self-control perseverance, to perseverance godliness, to godliness brotherly kindness, and to brotherly kindness love. For if these things are [ours] and abound, [we] *will be* neither barren nor unfruitful in the knowledge of our Lord Jesus Christ."

We have to learn to feed our faith and let it grow.

We have to learn to feed our faith and let it grow. Many times, we have faith but are in need of perseverance. Hebrews 6:12 says, "That you do not become sluggish, but imitate those who through faith and patience inherit the promises."

Then there are times when we have faith but are in need of love. Galatians 5:6 tell us that faith works through love. So always remember to let your faith grow strong. Seek the principles of God's Word. Make a faith movie for it builds your hope, and faith is the substance of things you hope for. Hope is a picture of the end result of receiving the promise of God. If you've found a promise of healing for your body, and you've spoken what God's promise says concerning your body, then get hope working for you by "seeing" the promise come true with the eyes of the spirit and faith.

The third key in the life of Abraham was that he gave glory to God. We have to learn to testify before the manifestation of the desired result. When we testify, it's proof that the manifestation is on the way. Giving glory to God before seeing the manifestation is like a woman who is pregnant and knows in nine months time that a child will be born. It's not presumption. It's a receiving of the supernatural seed of God's Word which has the power to produce.

The fourth key in Abraham's life was his conviction that God was able to do what He said He would do. This is the picture of the faithfulness of God. Abraham had a right image in his spirit about God. He knew the character of God—that God is good and faithful. He understood God wanted to bless him and not curse him. We must learn that God is out to heal us and not to harm us. He is looking to and fro to see how He can come into our lives and cause us to live lives of divine health.

As we've examined the Scriptures, we've seen the importance of faith, the harm of unbelief, and the need to exercise and build our faith for healing. In the next chapter, we're going to go more in detail about faith in relation to healing when the tango factor is operating. I believe it will help you get a proper attitude towards healing and, in fact, bring healing to you. It will encourage you to receive from God. That's one of my desires as you read this book— to encourage you through Scripture to receive healing.

CHAPTER 9

Positions of Faith

"The centurion answered and said,
'Lord, I am not worthy that You should come under my roof.
But only speak a word, and my servant will be healed.
For I also am a man under authority . . .'"

MATTHEW 8:8-10

The African impala can jump to a height of over ten feet and cover a distance of greater than thirty feet. Yet these magnificent creatures can be kept in an enclosure in any zoo with a three-foot wall. The animals won't jump if they can't see where their feet will fall.

This is a great lesson for all believers: Never make a move if you can't see where you'll land. Of course, I'm not speaking of our natural ability to see. I'm speaking about seeing with the eyes of the spirit.

As we learned in a prior chapter, a believer doesn't walk with natural sight, but spiritual sight which is faith. When we exercise faith, spiritual sight, we can be freed from the flimsy enclosures of life that have trapped the work of God from being progressed in our lives.

To have faith is to open the eyes of the spirit that cause us to see the work of God. Physical optics aren't the instruments to perceive the things of the Spirit. The Bible says, Moses "endured as seeing Him who is invisible" (Hebrews 11:27). Moses didn't see with his natural eyes, but with his spiritual eyes.

All around us are radio and television waves. A receiver helps to change their invisible frequencies into something that is tangible, where we can see or hear the effect of those waves. In that same manner, our spirits are receivers of faith that tune into the blessings of God.

Ephesians 1:3 says, "May blessing (praise, laudation, and eulogy) be to the God and Father of our Lord Jesus Christ (the Messiah) who has blessed us *in Christ* with every spiritual (given by the Holy Spirit) blessing in the heavenly realm" (AMP). Faith transfers those things that are in our heavenly bank account to the place of our need. That is the reason faith is always honored because it displays that God exists and God rewards.

Yes, faith always pleases God. As we continue talking about faith in relation to healing, we're going to see that the biblical accounts of healing demonstrate three aspects of faith—the receiver's faith, the intercessor's faith, and the minister's faith.

Receiver's Faith

The receiver's faith is the faith a person has to approach Jesus to receive the fulfillment of her need. The gospel of Matthew records the account of two blind men who had faith to be healed. Here is the story as it appears in Matthew 9:27-30.

> When Jesus departed from there, two blind men followed Him, crying out and saying, "Son of David, have mercy on us!" And when He had come into the house, the blind men came to Him. And Jesus said to them, "Do you believe that I am able to do this?" They said to Him, "Yes, Lord." Then He touched their eyes, saying, "According to your faith let it be to you." And their eyes were opened.

We see here that the blind men had faith to be healed. They couldn't see all the miracles that had happened or even see where Jesus was, but they had ears that heard which produced faith inside their hearts. That faith spoke—"'Son of David, have mercy on us!'" You see faith always speaks, maybe not always verbally, but it will speak at least through its actions.

When Jesus met with the blind men, He asked a question—"'Do you believe I am able to do this?'" I always wondered why in the world Jesus asked a question like that. Of course, they must have believed He was able or they wouldn't have asked. It seems like a no-brainer! I'm sure the blind men felt quite silly being asked that question. But I believe the reason Jesus asked them what He did was to force them to use their mouths to ask *Him* for help, thereby acknowledging their belief that He did have the power to help them. You see, the blind men probably had to constantly confess their blindness. They did this, more than likely, throughout the day to beg for alms. Jesus was making them use the confession of their mouths, in this case, to bring about their healing.

The Scripture declares that life and death are in the power of the tongue (Proverbs 18:21), and so are things like blessings and curses, faith and fear, and even sickness and healing. With our mouths, we affirm our faith in God. With our mouths, we make confession of our beliefs, so with our mouths, we can establish our healing. And, consequently, we can maintain our healing by the verbal confession of our faith.

> **With our mouths, we make confession of our beliefs, so with our mouths, we can establish our healing.**

Once the blind men confessed with their mouths their belief in Jesus' ability to heal them, they were healed instantly as Jesus spoke the words that released healing virtue. He said to the two blind men, "'According to your faith let it be to you.'" Notice their healing was contingent upon the confession of their faith—the receiver's faith!

The woman with the issue of blood suffered for more than twelve years. The Scriptures record that she also got healed because she had faith. Obviously, she didn't always have faith. She had sought the help of physicians and spent all the money she had. She just kept getting worse, but by hearing of the miracles of Jesus, faith was birthed in her heart. She fed her faith by the confession of her mouth. The Bible says in Mark 5:28, "For she kept saying, If I only touch His garments, I shall be restored to health" (AMP).

Are you beginning to see a pattern here? Our mouths are key to our receiving anything from God. Our words paint pictures in our spirits of a desired result. The woman with the issue of blood created a picture with her repeated statement, "If I only touch His garments, I shall be restored to health." She surpassed all obstacles and went and touched the garment of Jesus. As soon as she touched the garment, the anointing was released upon her life, and she was made whole. Here, we see again she had faith, and her faith had a corresponding action.

Another note I want to observe is that many people touched Jesus and were healed, and many people were touched by Jesus and healed. It worked both ways, either Jesus touched them or they touched Him.

In order for faith to be activated, then, we see the confession of the mouth has to be in line with the principle of God's Word. Second Corinthians 4:13 says, "And since we have the same spirit of faith, according to what is written, *'I believed and therefore I spoke,'* we also believe and therefore speak." Again, the pattern is I believe and, therefore, I speak.

> **We must be like the blind men, believing God is able to empower and heal us, holding fast the confession of our faith—the receiver's faith.**

A person who has faith is never rejected by God. Often, we're faced with situations that are overwhelming, and we feel as if we have no strength to stand on God's Word. At times like these, we have to do everything in our power to believe that His strength will be made perfect in our weakness (2 Corinthians 12:9). We must be like the blind men, believing God is able to empower and heal us, holding fast the confession of *our* faith—the receiver's faith. And then, we'll receive that which we have asked of Him.

Also, at such points in life, we need people who are full of faith and the Holy Spirit to stand with us. There are many times I've felt like I couldn't see a way out even though I had seen great things that God had done in my own life. I thank God during those times that I had people who surrounded me—people who had faith for me. This is the second aspect of faith we see in the Scriptures.

Intercessory Faith

Intercessory means the middle person or mediator between two people. We're familiar with the term when speaking of prayer. Intercessory prayer is praying on behalf of someone else. We also say that Jesus is our Intercessor, which simply means that He is praying to the Father on our behalf, as we read in Hebrews 7:25— "Therefore He is also able to save to the uttermost those who come to God through Him, since He always lives to make intercession for them."

We have biblical evidence of times where faith wasn't in the person who needed healing, but it was found in someone else— some intermediary or intercessory person. Parents, for example, can have faith for their children. Friends can have faith for friends. The idea behind the tango factor is that faith has to be present somewhere, even if it isn't in the person needing healing. It simply must be present in someone on behalf of someone else.

A Roman centurion approached Jesus for the healing of his servant. He was a man who surprised Jesus. He wasn't like any other slave master. This centurion cared for his servant. Other masters would have left the sick servant to die, but there was something different about this Roman centurion. He loved the Jewish people. He even built a synagogue for them. When he came to Jesus he said, "Lord, my servant boy is lying at the house paralyzed *and* distressed with intense pains" (Matthew 8:6, AMP).

Jesus immediately responded, "I will come and restore him" (v. 7, AMP).

The centurion felt unworthy that Jesus should enter his house, but he also understood the principle of authority, so he responded to Jesus by saying, "'Lord, I am not worthy that You should come under my roof. But only speak a word, and my servant will be healed. For I also am a man under authority, having soldiers under me. And I say to this *one*, "Go," and he goes; and to another, "Come," and he comes; and to my servant, "Do this," and he does *it*'" (Matthew 8:8-9).

Jesus was blown away at this man's response for He said, "'Assuredly, I say to you, I have not found such great faith, not even in Israel!'" (Matthew 8:10). The centurion's faith—an intercessor's faith—resulted in the healing of his servant.

There are several other accounts in Scripture where intercessory faith brought about healing. I want to highlight several principles from the centurion's story, though, and a few of these from other accounts. I believe these principles will encourage us to have faith for the healing of others and to understand that sometimes others will have faith for our healing.

The first principle is *you can have faith for the healing of another*. The centurion had faith for his servant. This story says nothing about the faith of the servant. It's not even mentioned. Don't ever come under condemnation that only you require faith to be healed. I know times in my life I've received some surprise attacks which I wasn't prepared for, and they knocked me down completely. I had no faith to believe God because I was weak and vulnerable at the time. In those times, I realized that God brought people of faith to surround me with their faith for my healing and well-being. My healing wasn't up to my faith; it was dependent upon their faith.

> God brought people of faith to surround me with their faith for my healing and well-being. My healing wasn't up to my faith; it was dependent upon their faith.

Not only did the centurion have faith for his servant, but remember Jairus and the Greek, Syro-Phoenician woman? Jairus had faith for his daughter to be healed (Luke 8:41-56), and the Greek, Syro-Phoenician woman had faith for her daughter to be delivered from demons (Matthew 15:21-28). What about the four crazy friends who had faith for their paralytic friend to be made well (Mark 2:3-5)?

I want to encourage you, dear reader, that there are those around you who don't have any faith or trust in Jesus, but you can have faith for them and take them to Jesus. That might be the only way for them to receive Jesus as their Savior. Be encouraged in your faith for others; it can do wonders for others. And should you be a person who struggles with faith for your own situation or need, be encouraged because God has someone, maybe even some crazy friends who will exercise their faith to bring you in contact with Jesus—to receive what it is you need.

The second principle we see regarding intercessory faith is that *it doesn't matter who you are or who you are not with God; what matters is that you have faith in Him.* Romans 2:11 tells us that God doesn't show favoritism. We see this in the story of the centurion. He wasn't a Jew. He wasn't one of God's chosen people. The Syro-Phoenician woman wasn't a Jew either. These two individuals had no covenant with God like the Jews, yet they could activate faith and receive the promises of God. Realize that God is no respecter of persons but of faith. If a person is willing to trust God, God can work miracles and allow His glory to be displayed through that person.

> **If a person is willing to trust God, God can work miracles and allow His glory to be displayed through that person.**

The third principle is the principle of authority and submission. We need to realize that *God has given us authority and power over sickness and disease.* Remember, Jesus said, "'And these signs shall follow those who believe: in My name they will cast out demons; they will speak with new tongues; they will take up serpents, and if they drink anything deadly, it will by no means hurt them; they will lay hands on the sick, and they will recover'" (Mark 16:17-18). When we speak the Word of God, sickness will flee. When we're ministering healing to people, we can speak the Word and be confident that sickness will leave. When we're sick and in need of healing, we can speak the Word and sickness will go.

The fourth principle is, even if you lose hope, *Jesus is out to deposit hope in your life to believe Him.* Romans 5:5 tells us, "Now hope does not disappoint us, because God's love has been poured into our hearts through the Holy Spirit which has been given to us." When Jairus had come to Jesus to ask Him to come to his house to lay hands on his daughter, Jesus immediately answered and was on His way. During that time, there was a break, where a woman with an issue of blood pressed through the crowd and reached out and touched the hem of His garment and was made whole. As this was happening, news came that Jairus's daughter was dead. As soon as Jesus heard the word that was spoken, He said to the ruler of the synagogue, "'Do not be afraid; only believe'" (Mark 5:36).

You see, this man would have been discouraged; once he heard his daughter was dead, he would have lost all hope. He might have been angry even, but Jesus encouraged him.

Situations may seem to get worse before they become better. Often, when ministering to people, we have to realize that we need to constantly encourage them to believe. We need to be like Jesus and feed them with encouragement to believe and trust. Remember this truth found in Job 14:7-9—"'For there is hope for a tree, if it is cut down, that it will sprout again, and that its shoots will not cease. Though its root may grow old in the earth, and its stump die in the ground, *yet* at the scent of water it will bud and bring forth branches like a plant.'" We have such a hope, even during our darkest hours. He is our Hope!

The fifth principle is *faith requires action*. When Jesus reached Jairus's house, everyone was weeping. Their response was a normal human response. But it wasn't the appropriate response to Jesus' words of encouragement—His words offering hope that she would live again. So when Jesus reached there, He sent everyone out of the room who didn't agree with Him. We read in Mark 5:40-42 that the people ridiculed Him, and so He put them out. Jesus, however, kept some with Him—namely, the mother and father, and those who were "with Him." He then took the little girl by the hand and spoke words to her, and she was raised up!

The sixth principle we see is *you'll need to fight on behalf of another*. Intercessory faith involves making every effort to see another person in need get to Jesus to receive from Him. When you have such faith, you need to realize that every obstacle, all demonic power, and harassing hosts are now against you and your helping the one in need.

> Intercessory faith involves making every effort to see another person in need get to Jesus to receive from Him.

The four crazy friends faced obstacles. They couldn't get to Jesus because of the crowds. They had to create a hole in the roof. The Syro-Phoenician woman was insulted as she was called a dog by Jesus. Imagine being insulted by Jesus. But she didn't get offended. She didn't get angry. She didn't waver in her petition. She was refused three times, but the fourth time when she corrected her motives and ways, Jesus answered her cry, and her daughter was delivered.

Just think of Jairus too. He was interrupted and delayed by another person who needed healing. Remember faith is a fight. When you decide to exercise faith, you'll be in a fight. When you're exercising faith for someone, you'll be in the fight on behalf of that person.

The last principle is *God's interested in wholeness, not just healing in part*. Never be disappointed when we approach God on behalf of someone that it didn't turn out the way you planned it. When the four friends approached Jesus with their friend, Jesus said to the paralytic that his sins were forgiven him. I'm sure at that time these four friends were totally taken back. They thought He would heal him, for they didn't see his need of forgive-

> When you decide to exercise faith, you'll be in a fight.

ness. Jesus saw that his greatest need was forgiveness of sin, so He forgave him and then healed him. If he was healed in body only, he still would have been headed for destruction. Jesus, however, took care of everything. He made him totally whole.

I'm reminded of a meeting where a man, who was lame in one leg, came limping to the altar. He desired to be healed. This man approached the evangelist and asked him to pray for him so that he might walk again on both feet. The evangelist looked at him and said, "Do you want to take the opportunity to have Jesus forgive you of your sins, and you can make Him your Lord and Savior?"

The man looked at the evangelist and said, "Sir, I'm tired of walking with a limp. I want to only walk all right."

The evangelist said, "At least right now you are only limping to hell, but when you get healed, you will be running to hell. Jesus not only wants to heal your body but your total being."

How true! Dear intercessor, God is interested in wholeness.

Minister's Faith

The minister's faith is the faith found in the person ministering healing. There are times when a person in need doesn't have faith, as we discussed previously. At the same time, however, there may be no one around him who has intercessory faith. But thank God for ministers, for those who can minister healing to a person because they're serving as a conduit of God's compassion and power.

I know this seems similar to the intercessory faith. The difference here is I'm talking about the faith of a person who is anointed to minister healing to the people in need. Remember faith and anointing have to make contact for the manifestation of the promise. The person ministering may have developed faith for healing by spending time in the Word of God, or the individual may have been graced with the gift of faith by the Holy Spirit. Such a one may release healing as he's used by the Holy Spirit. I recall reading about Smith Wigglesworth who would break people's crutches and canes as he said, "Be healed in the name of Jesus."

Often God uses people with the gift of healing so that it becomes a way maker for people to come and receive Jesus. Peter is a great example of this. Let's look at Acts 9:32-35. It reads:

As Peter traveled about the country, he went to visit the saints in Lydda. There he found a man named Aeneas, a paralytic who had been bedridden for eight years.

"Aeneas," Peter said to him, "Jesus Christ heals you. Get up and take care of your mat." Immediately Aeneas got up. All those who lived in Lydda and Sharon saw him and turned to the Lord (NIV).

Two whole cities were impacted as people turned to the Lord because of this healing.

In our next chapter, we're going to continue to look at the important role of our faith and its confession.

CHAPTER 10

Faith & the Power of the Tongue

"And since we have the same spirit of faith,
according to what is written 'I believed and therefore I spoke,'
we also believe and therefore speak."

2 CORINTHIANS 4:13

A man working in the produce department was asked by a lady if she could buy half of a head of lettuce. He replied, "Half a head? Are you serious? God grows these in whole heads and that's how we sell them!"

"You mean," she persisted, "that after all the years I've shopped here, you won't sell me half a head of lettuce?"

"Look," he said, "if you like, I'll ask the manager."

She indicated that would be appreciated, so the young man marched to the front of the store. "You won't believe this, but there's a lame-brained idiot of a lady back there who wants to know if she can buy half a head of lettuce."

He noticed the manager gesturing and turned around to see the lady standing behind him, obviously having followed him to the front of the store. "And this nice lady was wondering if she could buy the other half," he concluded.

Later in the day, the manager cornered the young man and said, "That was the finest example of thinking on your feet I've ever seen! Where did you learn that?"

"I grew up in Grand Rapids, and if you know anything about Grand Rapids, you know that it's known for its great hockey teams and its ugly women."

The manager's face flushed, and he interrupted, "My wife is from Grand Rapids!"

"And which hockey team did she play for?" (*10,000 Sermon* "Speech—Tongue").

God in His wisdom gave us a pair of legs, hands, ears, eyes, and yet only one tongue. And from the opening story, we should be grateful that He only gave us one tongue. It seems to be able to create enough trouble on its own.

Our tongue has tremendous power. With it we can bless, encourage, and strengthen others; and with it, we can curse, discourage, and destroy others.

In James 3, the tongue's power is compared to a bit in a horse's mouth and also a rudder on a ship (vv. 3-5). As a bit in a horse's mouth can turn the entire body of a horse, and as a ship's rudder can change the entire course of a ship, so can your tongue change the entire course of your life.

How does the tongue affect change in our lives? Through its power to confess or to command.

Power to Confess

The Greek word for *confess* is *homologeo* (Strong, "Greek Dictionary of the New Testament," 52), which means to speak in accordance with or to speak the same thing. When we confess something, we're speaking in accordance with what someone else has said.

We know as Christians we must confess things that are in line with the Word of God. But, if we're honest, we have to admit we sometimes confess things that are contrary to the Word of God. The content of what we confess depends upon us. We must choose to always confess—speak in accordance with—the Word of God. When we choose to have our confession line up with the Word of God, our spirits, souls, and bodies begin to agree with what the Word of God says, and we see the fruit promised in the Scriptures.

First John 1:9 says, "If we confess our sins, He is faithful and just to forgive us *our* sins and to cleanse us from all unrighteousness." When we confess a sin, we're simply agreeing with God about what we have done wrong. We're saying the same thing about sin as God does. When this happens, forgiveness is released.

There's a difference, however, between an honest confession motivated by godly sorrow and repentance *and* negative confession motivated by condemnation or shame. To constantly talk about how sinful and unworthy we are isn't what we should do. In Christ, "there is therefore now no condemnation" (Romans 12:1). Things from our pasts that have been confessed have also been forgiven. We shouldn't walk around allowing the enemy to make us feel insecure, shamed, and condemned. No, true confession of sin— saying the same thing God says about our sin—should lead to the release of forgiveness. Then we should continue that confession with what God says about us and who we are in Christ Jesus.

The foundation of receiving salvation is based on the principle of faith and confession.

The foundation of receiving salvation is based on the principle of faith and confession. The Bible declares in Romans 10:9-10 "that if you confess with your mouth the Lord Jesus and believe in your heart that God has raised Him from the dead, you will be saved. For with the heart one believes unto righteousness, and with the mouth confession is made unto salvation." The very way we entered into the abundant life is the very way we maintain and grow in our walks with God.

Concerning healing, 1 Peter 2:24 says, ". . . by whose stripes you were healed." Notice the past tense used in the verse. So when we're facing sickness, we must use our mouths to confess, "I'm healed in the name of Jesus Christ." It's not lying to do so; it's actually saying the same thing the Word of God says about our bodies. It's agreeing with the Word of God so that we see the desired end.

You might say, "Well, I don't feel like I should say that because the Bible says that you must have faith before you speak as it says in 2 Corinthians 4:13—'*I believed and therefore I spoke.*'" That's true, but only in part. The Bible also says in Romans 10:17 that faith comes by hearing the Word of God. So when you open your mouth and confess—saying the same thing as—the Word of God, faith will be produced. We must realize that confession of God's Word is necessary to produce faith and also release faith.

Confession producing faith involves speaking God's promises over a particular situation in our lives. We must work hard at this, as the Devil will attack the Word and do all that he can do to make us feel uninspired, mechanical, legalistic, and stupid. But just keep going and press through. Read the Word. Meditate on the Word. Speak the Word.

Confessing the Word of God to produce faith isn't an easy route. Your carnal mind wants to take the way of least resistance. Your carnal nature doesn't like things that require work. The carnal nature says to use every shortcut available.

Determine in your heart now to take the route of the Word of God. Your carnal nature doesn't need any training to claim sickness. You don't have to work hard at all to claim sickness. That's why you hear people say things like, "I'm coming down with a cold," "The flu season is here; I'll probably get it soon," or "Cancer runs in my family, so I'll probably have it someday."

Remember Proverbs 17:27—"He who has knowledge spares his words, and a man of understanding has a cool spirit" (AMP). Be cool and keep your mouth in line with the Word of God. Train your tongue to speak and agree with the Word of God. Training takes time. Training is hard work. But training will produce the habit of using your tongue to confess God's Word.

Power to Command

The second power of the tongue is to command. To command means to exercise authority or order things in place. The Bible says in Proverbs 18:21, "Death and life are in the power of the tongue, and they who indulge in it shall eat the fruit of it [for death or life]" (AMP). We've heard this verse often and know we have a choice to either speak life or death. There are times when it is appropriate to speak life to a situation, and there are times when it's appropriate to speak death.

Perhaps you've been taught as some have that, when Proverbs 18:21 talks about speaking life, it's addressing times you speak healing, blessing, and encouragement. And speaking death is when you gossip, criticize, tear down, judge, etc. But that's not the true essence of this verse.

In the life of Jesus, we find that Jesus used His tongue to release both life and death. We know many examples of life, but also we need to remember other occasions when He spoke death. I can think of one time in particular—when He spoke to the tree and cursed it (Matthew 21:19). There are times we, too, should speak death and not life. When I pray for the sick, for example, and see someone with a cancer or tumor, I command death to that sickness and then speak life to the part of the body that contained the tumor.

> . . . the core of our responsibility as believers is to lay hands on the sick and heal.

We've been given the authority to command by the Word of God. The Word of Lord declares that God commanded us to have dominion over everything on this earth except people. This includes our having dominion over sickness. Command it to leave your body or the body of one who is sick. Jesus commanded the winds to obey Him and be still. Jesus commanded dead bodies to come to life. Jesus commanded fever to leave a body. Jesus didn't pray for healing; He simply healed the sick. Only in James are we commanded to pray for the sick, and that responsibility is given to elders of the church, but the core of our responsibility as believers is to lay hands on the sick and heal.

I want to encourage you to open your mouth and speak to the sickness. Remember Mark 11:23—"Truly I tell you, whoever says to this mountain, be lifted up and thrown into the sea! And does not doubt at all in his heart but believes that what he says will take place, it will be done for him" (AMP).

As much as we speak life to things, we need to learn to curse those things that are not part of the Kingdom of God. We need to curse and speak death to sickness and disease. You have power to command and bring order.

As we close this section of teaching on faith, we'll now move to a discussion of the key ingredients and principles outlined in the Scriptures to receiving healing.

PART III

Receiving &
Ministering Healing

CHAPTER 11

Learning to Receive from God

"Until now you have asked nothing in My name.
Ask, and you will receive that your joy may be full."

JOHN 16:24

For this topic, I'm reminded of another story. Please excuse its seeming lack of spiritual significance, but I believe it conveys an important point in a humorous way.

A couple was celebrating their twenty-five years of marriage and also celebrating the husband's sixtieth birthday. During the party, the couple went for a walk on some trails behind their house when, suddenly, they tripped over a bottle and a genie came out. The genie offered to grant a wish to the husband and wife.

The woman said, "We've been so poor all these years, and I never got to see the world. I wish we could travel all over the world."

The genie waved his hand and—POOF!—the woman had millions of dollars and first class plane tickets in her hands.

Next, it was the man's turn. He paused for a moment and then said, "Well, I'd like to be married to a woman thirty years younger than me" (*10,000 Sermon* "Expectations—Marriage").

The genie waved his hand and—POOF!—the man was ninety!

Wow! I wouldn't like to be the man in that story. But I think we sometimes think God will do something similar to us as the genie did to the man in the story.

How many people are afraid to ask God for something, thinking that when God answers they'll receive something they didn't want. Jesus said, though, "Ask in my name, according to my will, and he'll most certainly give it to you. Your joy will be a river overflowing its banks" (John 16:24, MSG).

When we go before God with our needs, we'll receive answers that will produce joy. It's that easy to receive from God. Throughout the Bible, we find stories of people who approached God for a need in their lives and walked away with tremendous joy because He met their need.

When it comes to healing, we shouldn't fear or be uncomfortable. The Bible says healing is our bread. The Bible is full of healing stories that give us principles to help us receive from God. These principles are not an end in themselves, but each one will help us prepare our hearts to receive healing. If you are sick, please don't stop taking medication as you follow these principles. Every year we hear news of people dying as they did not seek medical treatment because of their beliefs. Don't deny the reality of sickness. Along with medication, practice these ten principles from God's Word.

Principle 1:
Develop a Biblical Image of God

It's important for us to develop a biblical image of God. God is good, and everything that is good comes from Him. I'm aware some individuals struggle with God's goodness. They think, *If God really is so good, then why do bad things happen?* But our questions and lack of understanding don't change the truth—God is good!

I'm reminded of the parable of the talents in the book of Matthew. The master in the story is a type of Christ. The servants are representative of believers like you and me. In the story, the Master called three people and, according to their ability, gave them talents—pieces of silver or gold. To one, he gave five talents, to another two, and to another one, and then he went into a far country. After awhile, the master returned and asked for an accounting of what he had given the three. The first two, the person with five talents and two talents respectively, increased in what was given because they invested their talents, but the third one with one talent went and hid the talent in the ground and did not have any increase. Matthew 25:24 tells us, "He who had received one talent also came forward, saying, Master, I knew you to be a harsh *and* hard man, reaping where you did not sow, and gathering where you had not winnowed [the grain]" (AMP). This servant had a wrong image of his master, and as a result, he failed to invest and, ultimately, failed to receive his reward.

How much are we like this latter servant—our image of God askew as it's been affected by the negative experience of others, by misinformed teaching that others have given us, or even by our own failure to see the promise of God come to pass. I want to assure you that our image of God doesn't need to be based on our circumstance or experiences, but solely on God's Word and God's character.

I was moved at Corrie Ten Boom's testimony of God's goodness for she said, "Deep in our hearts we believe in a good God. Yet how shallow is our understanding of His goodness, especially since we see many things that seem to deny it" (*10,000 Sermon* "Love of God"). Corrie Ten Boom clarified the issue for us as she continues:

> Often I have heard people say, "How good God is! We prayed that it would not rain for our church picnic, and look at the lovely weather!" Yes, God is good when He sends good weather. But God was also good when He allowed my sister, Betsie, to starve to death before my eyes in a German concentration camp. I remember one occasion when I was very discouraged there. Everything around us was dark, and there was darkness in my heart. I remember telling Betsie that I thought God had forgotten us. "No, Corrie," said Betsie, "He has not forgotten us. Remember His Word: 'For as the heavens are high above the earth, so great is His steadfast love toward those who fear Him.'"

Corrie concludes, "There is an ocean of God's love available—there is plenty for everyone. May God grant you never to doubt that victorious love—whatever the circumstances."

Yes, dear reader, get a true picture of who God is. He is altogether lovely. He is our Father, and He is a good, loving, giving Father. In fact, Jesus said, "'Do not fear, little flock, for it is your Father's good pleasure to give you the kingdom'" (Luke 12:32). I really want you to lay hold of the consistency, faithfulness, and goodness of the character of God. Perhaps a story about C.H. Spurgeon will help here.

> . . . lay hold of the consistency, faithfulness, and goodness of the character of God.

One day Spurgeon was walking through the English countryside with a friend. As they strolled along, the evangelist noticed a barn with a weather vane on its roof. At the top of the vane were these words—"God is love." Spurgeon remarked to his companion that he thought this was a rather inappropriate place for such a message. "Weather vanes are changeable," he said, "but God's love is constant."

"I don't agree with you about those words, Charles," replied his friend. "You misunderstood the meaning. That sign is indicating a truth: Regardless of which way the wind blows, God is love."

God is unchanging. His love is unchanging towards us. If we look again at the Greek, Syro-Phoenician woman's story, we see how her image of God was critical to the deliverance of her daughter. This woman didn't have any covenant rights like the Jews. As a matter of fact, Jesus asked the disciples to send her away and also insulted her by calling her a dog. But she must have known the character of God. She didn't get discouraged or bitter, but she persevered in her faith. She said to Jesus, "'Even the dogs eat the crumbs that fall from their master's table'" (Matthew 15:27, NIV). Her request was humble, fervent, desperate, worshipful, persevering, determined, and full of faith in Christ.

How did Jesus respond to her? He said, "'Woman, you have great faith! Your request is granted'" (v. 28, NIV). And her daughter was then healed. You see, she had a proper image of God. She knew her position as undeserving and without legal covenant rights like the Jews, yet she knew even the dogs had some rights—rights to the crumbs that the master throws away or gives to them. Children had enough bread to spare, so she claimed the scraps for her daughter. She knew that, although she was undeserving, God was a giving God. God was a loving God. God was a God of justice.

My friend, I want to encourage you that, if you have any needs in your life, approach God with confidence, assured He is a loving, giving, and caring Father.

My friend, I want to encourage you that, if you have any needs in your life, approach God with confidence, assured He is a loving, giving, and caring Father. Open the Scriptures and let the Holy Spirit teach you about the Father—about His love, mercy, power, and generosity. May you come to a similar revelation that the debtor did in the story below.

There was a man over $100,000 in debt. In our day, his debt would be more like $2,000,000. This debtor went to the king and asked if he could help him financially but didn't tell the king the amount. The king told him to go to the treasurer with his seal and ask him for what he wished. So he went and asked for $100,000. The treasurer sent word to the king to find out if such a large amount was acceptable. No one up until that time had asked such a large request. The king replied to the treasurer, "Pay the money at once. The philosopher has done me a singular honor. By the largeness of his request, he shows that he has understood both my wealth and generosity."

Wow! We need to approach God in the same manner so that our asking reveals we understand just who He is to us. As Jesus said to the woman at the well in John 4:10, "'If you knew the gift of God and *who* it is that asks you for a drink, you would have asked him and he would have given you living water'" (NIV).

Principle 2:
Develop a Biblical Self-image

We need to develop a proper image about ourselves. We need to realize that we're candidates to receive from God. Yes, the truth is we don't deserve anything we have ever received from Him—not salvation, not healing, not one blessing! But thanks be to God for His great grace—His unmerited favor—and for the fact that we don't get what we deserve!

Satan always tries to hinder people from approaching God.

Satan always tries to hinder people from approaching God. One of the ways he does this is by planting seeds of unbelief and unworthiness into their minds and hearts. Many have believed the Devil's lies that a certain state of moral excellence must be met before coming to God. "You've sinned," Satan says. "Don't go to church. For sure, don't let anybody know," he speaks condemnation to our souls. "If Christians knew what you were really like, they probably wouldn't let you worship with them," continues the Accuser of the brethren. "People don't like you because you smoke. They smell the cigarettes on your breath. They know you've been smoking." With such a grievous attack, his victims begin to think they're not worthy to receive anything from God. If they're not careful, they start to believe his lies about approaching their Father.

I would remind you of one of my favorite verses found in John 6:37. Jesus says, "'The one who comes to Me I will by no means cast out.'" No matter what lie Satan may be throwing at you, don't listen to him. You matter to God. More than you matter to your family, your church, or anyone else, you matter to God. When the days are hard, it's tough to remember that before you mattered to anyone else, you mattered to God. He knew you first. He's seen your whole life from beginning to end. He's known your potential and created you to fulfill it. He's known what it is to be you, to face what you face, to feel what you feel, because He put on frail humanity for you.

Remember, we come to the Father so that He can clean us up. We're unable to clean up ourselves. We need the help of Jesus and the Holy Spirit to overcome the world, the Devil, and the ungodly desires of our own flesh. God is easy to talk to. God is easy to recognize. He is easy to understand because we have the Holy Spirit as our Teacher. And He is easy to approach. Jesus' blood has paved the way for you and me to come boldly into the throne room of God. We must always keep in mind God's attitude towards us—"For I know the thoughts that I think toward you, says the Lord, thoughts of peace and not of evil, to give you a future and a hope" (Jeremiah 29:11).

When a person has a proper image about themselves, as painted in the Word of God, then that person can have hope. Someone has said, "If you expect nothing, you will get nothing." An environment of expectancy is a great place to put action to your faith. An environment of expectancy also creates boldness to approach God and make your requests known.

Principle 3:
Be Obedient to God

The third principle in receiving from God is to bring your life into obedience. Obedience is essential to healthy living. Jesus said that, if we love Him, then we'll obey His commands. He, of course, is the perfect example of obedience. Hebrews 5:8 says that "though He was a Son, *yet* He learned obedience by the things which He suffered." Through obedience the work of redemption was completed. So in the same manner, through obedience, the blessings of the finished work of redemption are also received.

John the disciple wrote, "Dear friends, if our hearts do not condemn us, we have confidence before God and receive from him anything we ask, because we obey his commands and do what pleases him" (1 John 3:21-22, NIV). This Scripture offers us three thoughts that we need to apply to our lives regarding obedience.

When John said, ". . . if our hearts do not condemn us . . . ," he was talking about there not being any unconfessed sin, the guilt of which could steal our confidence before God. Sin will hinder us from receiving from God. The psalmist says, "If I regard iniquity in my heart, the Lord will not hear" (Psalm 66:18). Harboring sin blocks us from receiving from God. We all go through periods in life when someone does us wrong, when we're mistreated or misunderstood, etc. It's one thing to get hurt by people; it's another thing to allow the effects of those hurts to settle in our hearts. We must not allow the fruit of unforgiveness—like hatred, bitterness, resentment, anger, and other pent-up emotions—to get into our spirits and ultimately find expression in our bodies.

We must not allow the fruit of unforgiveness—like hatred, bitterness, resentment, anger, and other pent-up emotions—to get into our spirits and ultimately find expression in our bodies.

It's a known fact that some tense or frightened people may suffer from stomach disorders, anxious people from ulcers, and contentious and fractious people from arthritis, bone disease, or aching joints. Though not all people who have these aforementioned sicknesses may be a direct result from the things I've mentioned, science has found that many sicknesses and diseases stem from such unresolved issues.

I've personally seen some in meetings who have been harboring unforgiveness for years, and as they release it, the healing process starts in their lives without their even receiving prayer. Over the years, I've realized that many who come for healing actually go home with their sickness. We've prayed with all our might, faith, and confidence in God, yet these have walked away sick. I've found that their unwillingness to release things from their lives, to free their hearts from the condemnation of sin, is what has been in the way.

Remember, John said we need to obey God's commands. One of His commands involves our forgiving others just as He forgave us. But in relation to receiving healing, God might tell us to do something just as He instructed individuals like King Hezekiah, Naaman, and Miriam. Each of these was told what he or she needed to do in order to receive healing. I'm convinced that for each one of us there is a different condition that needs to be obeyed in order to position ourselves to receive healing from God. For some of us, it may be getting our finances in order, for some it may be getting our relationships in order, and for others it may be simply gaining self-control and putting anger to death in our lives.

Bringing our lives into obedience with God's commands and Word will open the door for us to walk in blessing. Remember what God told the Israelites? He spoke through Moses and said, "'If you fully obey the Lord your God and carefully follow all his commands I give you today, the Lord your God will set you high above all the nations on earth. All these blessings will come upon you and accompany you if you obey the Lord your God'" (Deuteronomy 28:1-2, NIV).

Looking at verse 15 of the same chapter in Deuteronomy, we see that walking in disobedience will result in "all these curses" to "come upon" us. It's as simple as it gets. Jesus has finished the work on the cross to make us righteous, so we need to learn to live and rest in that finished work by hearing the voice of God and obeying His command with the help of the Holy Spirit.

Finally, John's last thought is for us to do what pleases God. Your obedience should stem from a right motive. We should want to do what's right, not just to get what we want, but because we truly want to please our Father. When Jesus visited Peter's house and found that his mother-in-law was sick, Jesus "touched her and the fever left her, and she got up and began to serve Him" (Matthew 8:14). This is a great illustrative truth. God's healing in your life should cause you to rise up and serve Him. Sadly, I've seen many with a wrong motive in their hearts. They've wanted healing, yet refused to continue to live lives that please God.

> God's healing in your life should cause you to rise up and serve Him.

The Lord Jesus always did what was pleasing to the Father (John 8:29). At the same time, He didn't live selfishly to please

Himself (Romans 15:3). His life was entirely determined by the will of God for Him, and in carrying out that will, He found pleasure (John 4:34; 5:30; 6:38) and pleased God.

The concept of pleasing God was especially important for the apostle Paul. Indeed, it was the goal and controlling ambition of his life, for, as he writes to the church in Corinth, "We make it our goal to please Him, whether we are at home in the body or away from it" (2 Corinthians 5:9, NIV). Only a believer indwelt by the Spirit can please God, for "those who are in the flesh cannot please God" (Romans 8:8).

Principle 4:
Be Specific in your Requests

The fourth principle that is important in receiving from God is learning to be specific in our requests and create an environment where God can move. Someone has said, "Vague prayers receive vague answers; specific prayers receive specific answers."

Be specific about your condition and your expected results. The reason I always encourage this isn't so much for God to know; He knows already before we even ask or think to ask. No, being specific in our requests helps us to recognize when we receive our answer so that we can give glory to God. Over the years, I've learned we can actually miss God's answer because we weren't specific. I've seen God meet people, and later these have become convinced that what had happened wasn't God; it was just their own strength, wisdom, or sheer happenstance that changed their circumstance. Being specific helps us "know that we know" God met us.

Whenever I'm facing a crisis in any area, especially when it comes to health issues, I usually get on my computer and print out a list of healing Scriptures and get in bed and read those Scriptures over and over again. At first this may seem only an exercise of the mind, but at some point the truth of these words will begin to enter my heart and a personal revelation will come.

I've also made a custom audio CD of healing Scriptures gathered from various sources along with praise and worship songs that speak about receiving from God, the goodness of God, healing, and other things that will help me line up with God's purpose. I play those music CDs over and over again until their message gets into my spirit. It's amazing how much easier it is for me to take my eyes off the sickness and look at God and His character. It helps me to bring my thoughts, my plans, my actions, my attitude, and everything I am in submission to God and His will. It even assists me in helping phrase my requests in prayer.

When you're sick, start recollecting all the times God brought about a victory for you and build an environment where your faith can touch the power of God. Faith speaks. And faith works on specific requests. Begin to speak what you believe and not what you're feeling. The healing is in your mouth. The miracle is in your mouth.

Principle 5:
Continue to be Thankful

One of the great things I learned from my dad is the power of thanksgiving. He always says, "In the natural world, you say *thank you* after you receive something, but in the spiritual world you say *thank you* before you receive the manifestation of your answer." There is great truth in that. Faith sees the invisible. Faith is the evidence of things hoped for. Faith helps us to be persistently thankful because we see what we've hoped for and are waiting for the manifestation of it.

Some people I know suggest that, once the prayer of faith has been prayed, it's not necessary to be concerned about that matter anymore for it's in God's hand. Yes, once we pray, we commit what we've prayed for to Him. But that doesn't mean we should stop asking Him.

In fact, there are times when we need to persevere in prayer because of the enormous opposition sent by the enemy to cause us to give up and doubt. We know it's possible to be full of faith for a particular situation and yet not be healed instantaneously because healing can come gradually. We know God will be faithful to His Word if we're faithful to believe! It is written, "Do not become sluggish, but imitate those who through faith and patience inherit the promises" (Hebrews 6:12). When Jesus taught the disciples, He told them to ask and they would receive (Matthew 7:7). The word *ask* is in a continuous tense, meaning to go on asking or to continue asking. There is perseverance required on our side, as Hebrews 10:35-36 affirms: "Therefore do not cast away your confidence, which has great reward. For you have need of endurance, so that after you have done the will of God, you may receive the promise."

Along with perseverance we need an attitude of thankfulness. The apostle Paul wrote, "Do not be anxious about anything, but in everything, by prayer and petition, with thanksgiving, present your requests to God. And the peace of God, which transcends all understanding, will guard your hearts and your minds in Christ Jesus" (Philippians 4:6-7, NIV).

Thanksgiving keeps our minds renewed. Thanksgiving guards our hearts from any fiery darts of the enemy. Again, I want to be clear in saying that, when we're talking about thanksgiving, we're not talking about thanksgiving for what we have already received. We're talking about thanksgiving before we receive. The fact is we need to be persistently thankful before and through the process of getting our needs met.

The fact is we need to be persistently thankful before and through the process of getting our needs met.

Giving thanks for the answer before the miracle or healing is manifested was also something Jesus practiced. We know that, when Jesus prayed over the loaves and fish before feeding the multitudes, He "gave thanks" to His Father. Thanksgiving preceded the miracle. And when Jesus went to Bethany to raise up Lazarus from the dead, He went to the place where Lazarus's dead body was kept. He told the people to remove the stone, and when He prayed He said, "'Father, I thank you that you have heard me'" (John 11:41, NIV). Again thanksgiving preceded the miracle.

Many people wait until they receive the answer to be thankful, but we need to strive to practice what should be common to us, for it says in Colossians 2:6-7—"So then, just as you received Christ Jesus as Lord, continue to live in him, rooted and built up in him, strengthened in the faith as you were taught, and *overflowing with thankfulness*" (NIV). Thanksgiving and prayer always go together. And so do rejoicing and prayer—"Be joyful always; pray continually; give thanks in all circumstances, for this is God's will for you in Christ Jesus" (1 Thessalonians 5:16-18, NIV).

An attitude of thanksgiving in prayer before the need is met raises our expectation and confidence, knowing that God will hear us and answer us. The apostle Paul said, "But thanks be to God! He gives us the victory through our Lord Jesus Christ" (1 Corinthians 15:57). Also another verse that I keep in mind is Philippians 4:4—"Rejoice in the Lord always. I will say it again: Rejoice!" (NIV). Rejoicing in the Lord is faith expressed, knowing that God's power is released into the situation to free us from any difficulty. It's unlikely to see much of His power released into the situation without the spirit of rejoicing and thanksgiving.

Principle 6:
Get in the Path of God

We need to practice getting in the path of God. When we need to receive from God, we have to get into His path and the channels of His power. Zacchaeus did this when he climbed up a tree that was on the path Jesus was taking. The woman with the issue of blood heard that Jesus was passing by, so she pressed through the crowds just so that she could get in His path and touch the hem of His garment. The blind man heard that Jesus was passing by, so he opened his mouth and shouted in order to have Jesus come to him. After Jesus ascended, people looked to get into the pathway of some of His disciples like Peter, hoping that they could receive a touch from God.

At this point, I'm reminded of something that's critical here. If

God is doing a work in your church, don't go somewhere else. The woman who had a spirit of infirmity and was bent over and could in no way raise herself up for over eighteen years was found in the house of God (Luke 13:10-14). The man with a withered hand also was found in the house of God. One of the great blessings we have of being part of a local church is that we can call for the elders to pray for us (James 5:14-15).

If you're sick, then don't wait for someone to be led by God to come to you. Go to the house of God. But if you're so sick that you are unable to go, then pick up the phone and call the elders and ask them to pray for you. If you can't go to them, ask them to come to you and lay hands on you and anoint you with oil. If they can't come, then ask them to send a prayer cloth as a point of contact. Though some are skeptical about prayer cloths, Acts 19:11-12 contains an example of using these—"Now God worked unusual miracles by the hands of Paul, so that even handkerchiefs or aprons were brought from his body to the sick, and the diseases left them and the evil spirits went out of them." One day a lady called my dad from Switzerland who was ill for some time. She later became paralyzed and was in a wheelchair. Dad was in India that time and could not go pray for her, but He prayed over the phone and told her that he would send a prayer letter and a prayer cloth via mail. As soon as she received the envelope, she opened it with faith and came in agreement with the prayer written on the letter. She put her hand on the prayer cloth and was made whole, able to leave her wheelchair.

Principle 7:
Become a Giver

Giving is central to our receiving from God. We know this principle from Luke 6:38 where Jesus said, "'Give and it will be given to you.'" As believers, giving should thrill our hearts. I'm not talking about just giving of our finances, but our very lives should evidence hearts that give.

I must confess that there are times when I'm sick and I don't even feel like preaching, but I know that people need to hear the Word of God—in fact, I realize I need to hear it, too—and I go and preach anyway. I may even give an altar call, and being sick myself, I can question my own ability to pray for others when I'm sick myself. But I become a giver anyway. I preach and pray for the sick, investing in the lives of others. There have been times I've experienced personal healing while doing this.

When you are sick, the best thing to do is get your eyes off your sickness and get in the practice of giving to others. Start praying for others who are sick. One of the Beatitudes says, "'Blessed are the merciful, for they will be shown mercy'" (Matthew 5:7). The same principle is found in forgiveness, for we read, "'Forgive us our debts, as we also have forgiven our debtors'" (Matthew 6:12).

We should keep in mind that our giving isn't buying something from God; we can't buy the blessings of God. The blessing of God comes to us by His grace. Giving doesn't produce faith; it's an expression of faith that is in a heart. Giving enables us to receive from God. I tell people to sow a financial seed; it's not to produce faith, or buy healing. I encourage them to sow a financial seed as an act of faith, knowing that God is healing them. Sowing financial seeds opens our lives to receive from God. We're simply being obedient to the law of sowing and reaping. Remember, dear reader, God know the motives and intents of our hearts.

I think of the widow of Zarephath as an example. One day God came to Elijah and said to him to go down to Zarephath for there was a woman there who He had instructed to provide for Elijah. Elijah obeyed and went down to Zarephath. This woman had practically nothing left in her house, except a small portion of food. Yet Elijah taught her the power of giving. Let's look at the story for a moment.

> So he went to Zarephath. When he came to the town gate, a widow was there gathering sticks. He called to her and

asked, "Would you bring me a little water in a jar so I may have a drink?" As she was going to get it, he called, "And bring me, please, a piece of bread." "As surely as the Lord your God lives," she replied, "I don't have any bread—only a handful of flour in a jar and a little oil in a jug. I am gathering a few sticks to take home and make a meal for myself and my son, that we may eat it—and die." Elijah said to her, "Don't be afraid. Go home and do as you have said. But first make a small cake of bread for me from what you have and bring it to me, and then make something for yourself and your son. For this is what the Lord, the God of Israel, says: 'The jar of flour will not be used up and the jug of oil will not run dry until the day the Lord gives rain on the land.'" She went away and did as Elijah had told her. So there was food every day for Elijah and for the woman and her family. For the jar of flour was not used up and the jug of oil did not run dry, in keeping with the word of the Lord spoken by Elijah" (1 Kings 17:10-16, NIV).

A day that she had planned would be her last was turned around by God into the beginning of a relationship of faith and miracles. Not only did she learn this God of Israel was the One who would sustain her physically, but she came to know Him as the only true God. The lesson on the principle of giving is the same today as in Elijah's day. God wants us to be willing to give out of our abundance and share what He has blessed us with. Giving from what we have in abundance is the easiest way to be generous. But He also requires us to give out of our lack.

A couple in my church moved from India to the United States. They had filed for their green cards which would give them permanent residency status to stay in America. There was a long delay, and nothing seemed to be working. This couple knew a lot of families in the same situation. They prayed about their needs, and yet nothing seemed to be happening. So they decided that they would start giving by praying for other families who needed what they needed. They made a list of friends that had also filed for green cards, and they began to pray for them. As they became faithful in doing that, God honored them, and they received their green cards in a miraculous way.

Remember giving positions you to receive from God. When you're in need, plant a seed, and get ready for God to bring something into your life that you needed.

Principle 8:
Partake of Communion

For me the best point of contact to experience healing is when I partake of Holy Communion. When did you last receive Holy Communion? The church worldwide uses different terms like the Lord's Supper, the breaking of bread, or the Eucharist. The Catholics receive the Communion Meal at Mass on a weekly basis. Protestants may receive the Lord's Supper, or Communion, once a month or as infrequently as once a year. Many have forgotten or have belittled the power of breaking bread together. In the New Testament, it was very common to break bread in the *homes* of people; this seems to be a lost practice today.

There are so many differences in the beliefs about Holy Communion between the Catholics and Protestants. The Catholics participate in Mass in which the priest offers the bread and the wine called Eucharist. *Eucharist* simply means to give thanks in the Greek language. During Eucharist, the Catholics believe the bread becomes the literal body of Christ and the wine becomes the literal blood of Christ. This teaching in theological terms is called *transubstantiation*. The difficulty with this view is that it says the same sacrifice that Jesus offered on the cross is offered every time you take Communion.

The Lutherans believe in a doctrine called *consubstantiation*. This simply means that, in Communion, the bread and the cup of Communion coexist and are equal to the flesh and blood of Jesus, but still remain the bread and the wine. It's important that we have a proper view because, if we believe that the bread and the blood become the literal blood and body of Jesus and the sacrifice is being offered again and again, it means that the work of the cross isn't finished.

Many view a time of breaking bread simply as a sacrament or a religious duty to remember the death, burial, and resurrection of Jesus. However, there's more to it than that. Every time you participate in a time of Communion, you have access to what Christ obtained on the cross of Calvary for you.

Every time you break bread, it is a prophetic act by which the benefits of the work on the cross are ministered to you.

Every time you break bread, it is a prophetic act by which the benefits of the work on the cross are ministered to you. It gives you an opportunity to identify with the death, burial, and resurrection of Jesus Christ. When you identify with Him, the benefits are also released in your life. Every time we partake of the Communion, we encourage people to receive anything that is needed that the cross offers—anything like forgiveness, healing, canceling of curses, strength for any weakness, etc. Every time we partake, there should be an expectancy that the blessing of the finished work of the cross will be administered.

The apostle Paul when talking about the Holy Communion says that many believers are weak, sick, and die before their time because they don't discern the Lord's body—"For he who eats and drinks in an unworthy manner eats and drinks judgment to himself, not discerning the Lord's body. For this reason many *are* weak and sick among you, and many sleep" (1 Corinthians 11:29-30). Many have misinterpreted this verse by saying, if you have sin in your life, don't partake of Communion for that is partaking in an unworthy manner. That is wrong. with the truth is we may come with sin in our lives, but as we examine ourselves in the light of the Holy Spirit, Communion offers us an opportunity to repent of our sins and receive cleaning. To partake in an unworthy manner is to ignorantly take the bread and the cup of blessing without understanding the power of the meal that is shared. We need to keep in mind, that the blood of Jesus takes care of our sinfulness, and the bread that represents the physical body of Jesus takes care of our sicknesses, "by whose stripes you were healed" (1 Peter 2:24).

The discerning of the Lord's body has to do with the natural, physical body of Jesus—that Jesus was perfect, sinless human. He took sin, sickness, poverty, and all such things upon Him so that we might be made whole, righteous, and healed.

Discerning of the body also has to do with the spiritual Body of Jesus—the church. We're all members in need of each other and of Jesus our Head. It's important that we don't forsake the assembling of ourselves and that we maintain pure relationships with each another. If you know that something is wrong in your relationship with someone, than use the time of Communion to go and correct that relationship, because it's not a natural power uniting but God's power being released to unite us during Holy Communion. We're actually having communion with the Father and communion with members of the Body of Christ.

Whenever you are sick, you can receive healing in your body through the Communion Meal shared in your church or better yet in your home with your family together. I encourage you to make this a regular practice in your home so that you can receive the benefit of healing administered to your body. Remember that the communion meal deals with our sinfulness and our sickness. I want to encourage you to take the elements of Communion with faith. Let it administer its full blessing upon your life.

When taking Communion at home, I recommend doing the following:

- Open a portion of Scripture that talks about Communion.
- Meditate on Christ—look backward to the cross (His suffering, death, and burial); look upward to His resurrection and ascension to the right hand of the Father; and look forward to His soon return.

- Examine your life—allow the Holy Spirit to address your needs in light of the cross, and allow Him to deal with any sin.
- Give thanks for the elements—acknowledge what each element represents in Christ's personal work for you.
- Worship Him.
- Partake of the elements in faith.
- Pray for one another.

Principle 9:
Enlarge & Multiply your Blessing

In our previous study, we learned how to keep our healing from the story of the leper who was cleansed in Matthew 8. The leper was told to testify of his healing and go to the temple to see the priests. We likened that to giving testimony to glorify God and to being part of a local church where we can be fed, nourished, and enriched with the Word of God and fellowship with believers.

We not only need to keep our healing, but we need to learn how to enlarge, increase, and multiply the blessing of healing. The children of Israel were told by God, "'Every commandment which I command you today you must be careful to observe, that you may live and multiply, and go in and possess the land of which the Lord swore to your fathers'" (Deuteronomy 8:1). If God was going to bless them, then they needed to learn to live in the blessing and increase in it.

One of the ways to multiply your blessing is to give back to God what you've received. You might say, "How do I do that when I've received healing?"

The way to give it back to God is to let God use your blessing of healing to bring healing to others. If you've been healed, then God wants to use you to be a channel to heal others.

The Samaritan woman, when she received life from Jesus, went and proclaimed it to the whole town (John 4:28-30). The whole town came to see Jesus. You see, she multiplied the effectiveness of her blessing. When you're healed, it's important that you see the big picture—God wants to declare the Kingdom of God throughout the earth. Healing isn't just about you. Begin to testify to others of what God can do and let God use the testimony to bring hope and healing to others.

At one point in King David's life, as he was out in the wilderness, he longed for water and said, "'Oh, that someone would get me a drink of water from the well near the gate of Bethlehem'" (2 Samuel 23:15, NIV). The Philistines had their garrison in Bethlehem and were looking to kill David. Three mighty men, who were faithful to David, broke through the camp of the Philistines, drew water from the well of Bethlehem, and brought it to him. When David saw what these men had done, he took the drink and poured it out as an offering to the Lord. God blessed him for it and multiplied his blessing by giving him victory over the Philistines.

Elkanah, who was from the town of Ramathaim, had two wives. One was called Hannah and the other Peninnah. Peninnah bore children to Elkanah, but Hannah was barren. Because Peninnah was fruitful and saw that Hannah was barren, she consistently taunted Hannah, cruelly rubbing it in and never letting her forget that God had not given her children. In her desperation, Hannah cried out to the Lord, and the Lord answered her through Eli the priest who said, "'Go in peace, and may the God of Israel grant you what you have asked of him'" (1 Samuel 1:17, NIV). "So in the course of time Hannah conceived and gave birth to a son. She named him Samuel, saying, 'Because I asked the Lord for him'" (v. 20, NIV).

Hannah knew how to multiply her healing. She gave back Samuel to God for His use, and the Bible says in 1 Samuel 2:20-21—

Eli would bless Elkanah and his wife, saying, "May the Lord give you children by this woman to take the place of the one she prayed for and gave to the Lord." Then they would go home. And the Lord was gracious to Hannah; she conceived and gave birth to three sons and two daughters. Meanwhile, the boy Samuel grew up in the presence of the Lord.

Did you see that? Not only did she receive Samuel, but as she gave him back to the Lord, God blessed her womb. She multiplied her healing and received many more children.

Dear reader, if you have received anything from the Lord, learn to enlarge, increase, and multiply your blessing for the sake of the Kingdom of God. When Hannah gave the son back to the Lord, she thought that God would only use him to do some work in the temple, like cleaning the temple, lighting the golden lamp stand, changing the bread, or taking the offering. God had bigger things in mind. The Bible says that God established Samuel as a prophet to the nation of Israel (1 Samuel 3:19-21). You might be thinking only of getting healed from your sickness, but God's seeing something beyond you. He is looking not only to heal you but to use you.

Principle 10:
Build a Prayer Hedge of Protection

We need to learn to build a prayer hedge for protecting our healing. A physical wall or hedge can serve as a property boundary or even as a means of protection from intruders. The concept of a prayer hedge is the same—it's used as a boundary and as protection. We protect our healing by building a prayer hedge around our bodies and entire lives.

When a person builds a wall around a house or even a fence, he stops easy access to the property. In the same manner, when we build prayer hedges around our lives, we stop the intrusion of the enemy. We keep him from bringing symptoms of sickness or any form of evil that will cause sickness and bondage in our lives. For the house, the hedge might be built out of bricks, wood, or mortar but for our lives, the hedge is made from biblical materials. Here are some of the biblical materials we need to build a prayer hedge:

- The name of Jesus (Psalm 3:3).
- The blood of Jesus (Revelation 12:11).
- The house of God (Psalm 27:5).
- Angels (Psalm 34:7; 91:11).
- Faith (1 John 5:4; 1 Peter 5:9; Ephesians 6:16).
- Personal integrity (Psalm 25:19-21; 84:11).
- Sacrifice of praise and worship (Psalm 32:6-7).

I believe we need to consistently, through prayer, use these biblical materials to build prayer hedges. These will help us secure our lives in Christ and be free from the bondage of sickness and any form of evil.

There are six areas of our lives for which we need to build a prayer hedge:

- Our souls (Philippians 4:8; Romans 12:1-2; 2 Corinthians 10:3-5). We should pray for protection from division, poverty, unbelief, lust, unforgiveness, bitterness, envy, hatred, anger, strife, unworthiness, condemnation, idolatry, drunkenness, guilt, negativity, and confusion.
- Our physical bodies (Psalm 103:1-5). We should pray for protection from threats, accidents, disasters, attacks, assassination, sickness, and disease.
- Our spirits (Psalm 140:4-7). We should pray for protection from deceiving spirits, lying tongues, wounding people, woundedness, and bitterness.
- Our relationships (1 Thessalonians 3:12-13; 4:7; 1 Peter 1:15-16). We should pray for protection from sexual lust, sexual impurities, fantasies, and adultery.
- Our finances (Proverbs 3:9-10; Malachi 3:10-12; Psalm 41:1-3; Genesis 26:12; Deuteronomy 28:8). We should pray for the protection of our finances from emergency use, cheating, deception, and wrong investing.
- Our leaders (1 Timothy 2:1-2; Hebrews 13:7, 18; Colos-

sians 4:2-4). We should pray for the leaders and mentors in our lives—for their protection—including our bosses, pastors, cell leaders, city leaders, and national leaders.

CHAPTER 12

Ministering Healing

"Is anyone among you sick? Let him call
for the elders of the church, and let them pray over him,
anointing him with oil in the name of the Lord.
And the prayer of faith will save the sick,
and the Lord will raise him up.
And if he has committed sins, he will be forgiven."

JAMES 5:14-15

One of the most amusing things I've witnessed in the work of the ministry is seeing someone try to be "spiritual." If you've been a Christian for any amount of time, I'm sure you've seen it too. I'm *not* talking about someone being a hypocrite—someone who pretends to be something he's not. I'm talking about sincere Christian people who really love Jesus and are following hard after the principles of Christ—those who somehow feel they have to have a special aura of godliness, holiness, and spirituality about them. For example, when they stand behind the pulpit, they can't say God in a normal voice; they have to drag out the short vowel sound and punctuate the final consonant sound. They want to sound spiritual by using a certain tone of voice, by standing or walking a certain way, or by using certain words.

I'm sure you've seen someone like this before. I think we've all put on the Christian persona at one time or another in order to impress others. I think the more we spend time with the Holy Spirit, though, the more we realize that we don't have to try to be spiritual. In fact, God just made us naturally to be spiritual without ever changing the tone of our voices or the poise of our postures.

It's sad to say, but I believe even God's ministers are guilty of putting on airs. The temptation to impress and influence—to be taken more seriously or be viewed as more spiritual—may even be greatest among God's ministers. We have to learn that, when we're ministering in the power of God, it should be natural to us. Just because we change the tone of our voice, our words, or even have a certain posture doesn't mean any more power will flow through us.

One of the greatest privileges we have in our covenant with God is that we're partners with the Holy Spirit to accomplish the will of God. Since the Holy Spirit requires our bodies to do the work, our hands become His hands and our mouths become His mouth, and I would even go as far to say that according to Scripture our bodies are still His body. So while ministering to people, we must be aware that it's the Holy Spirit working in us and through us.

So while ministering to people, we must be aware that it's the Holy Spirit working in us and through us.

Jesus gave us a wonderful pattern to follow for living a daily life and ministering to people. John 5:19 records, "Then Jesus answered and said to them, 'Most assuredly, I say to you, the Son can do nothing of Himself, but what He sees the Father do; for whatever He does, the Son also does in like manner.'"

We have to learn to follow the leading of the Holy Spirit every time we minister to people. We can't just do things even if examples are found in the Scriptures. There are things that we have a direct command to practice, and some things that are written as examples to teach us a principle; in both cases, however, we need to follow the leading of the Holy Spirit.

The Scripture records many ways Jesus and the apostles ministered to people. We previously discussed how people took handkerchiefs, aprons, and clothing that had touched Paul's body. These they put it on the sick and saw illnesses cured and even saw some delivered from evil spirits. In the ministry of Peter, his very shadow falling on people brought healing. In the ministry of James, we have the elder of a local church anointing with oil and seeing the sick healed. In the ministry of Jesus, He spoke and commanded healing to manifest, He laid hands on the sick, and also He incorporated methods that were out of the ordinary, like spitting in the blind man's eyes. The more extraordinary methods must be approached cautiously and under the definite leading of the Spirit. We must not use these particular methods haphazardly; that is, just because Jesus did it does not give us the *right* to do likewise. Apart from the unction or anointing of the Holy Spirit, none of these methods will work for any of us.

I've heard people, who knew that Smith Wigglesworth punched a man and he was healed, start punching people. In their zeal, they thought Wigglesworth's method was a pattern for them to follow. I'm not saying these methods are wrong, but we need to be careful that we don't do things just for the sake of practice without having any direction from the Holy Spirit.

It's a privilege to be used by God. I love the verse that says, "'I tell you the truth, anyone who has faith in me will do what I have been doing. He will do even greater things than these, because I am going to the Father'" (John 14:12, NIV). We can expect God to use us in healing the sick and see more sickness and disease healed than Jesus saw when He was here on this earth. Amazing! Keep in mind, though, that God is the Source of the power; you and I are only the channels to release healing. "Now to him who is able to do immeasurably more than all we ask or imagine, according to his power that is at work within us" (Ephesians 3:20, NIV).

Looking at some examples in Scripture for healing, we find certain practices are evident that we can use today.

Use the Name of Jesus

The greatest name is the name of Jesus. The sweetest name is the name of Jesus. The most powerful name is the name of Jesus. The name of Jesus is our power of attorney for Kingdom privileges.

The Scriptures record some wonderful things regarding the power of Jesus' name. In Psalm 8:9, we read, "O Lord, our Lord, how excellent is Your name in all the earth!" The name of Jesus is our defense and strong tower, as Psalm 18:10 tells us—"The name of the Lord is a strong tower; the righteous run to it and are safe." Salvation and deliverance are found in the name of Jesus.

In the earthly ministry of Jesus, we see a demonstration of power and authority over disease, demons, death, and nature. Jesus did not have to argue with the problem or demons, but took authority over them. This same authority has been given to us! We have every right to use it, and we must start using it in a greater way to bring more glory to the Father.

In Acts 3, we see Peter using the authority of the name of Jesus.

Then Peter said, "Silver and gold I do not have, but what I do have I give you: In the name of Jesus Christ of Nazareth, rise up and walk." And he took him by the right hand and lifted *him* up, and immediately his feet and ankle bones received strength. So he, leaping up, stood and walked and entered the temple with them; walking, leaping, and praising God (vv. 6-7).

I'm reminded of a comment one pastor made while he was preaching from this text. He said, "Today the conditions are reversed—today's ministers are very pleased that they now have much silver and gold. They fail to realize that they have traded the power of God for silver and gold." Peter knew that the name of Jesus was more important than silver or gold, because it could provide healing as well as the silver and gold.

Our lives must not only reflect the life of Christ but also demonstrate the power of God as seen in the life of Christ. We must realize that the name of Jesus is all-powerful, and nothing can stand against it. We're to use the authority that Jesus has given us and come against the negatives in our lives.

Jesus has given us a name to use that is above every name or authority in the universe. Everything has to bow or yield to the name of Jesus. The name of Jesus is your power of attorney. Father God will honor the name of His Son, for Philippians 2:9-11 tells us, "Therefore God also has highly exalted Him and given Him the name which is above every name, that at the name of Jesus every knee should bow, of those in heaven, and of those on earth, and of those under the earth, and *that* every tongue should confess that Jesus Christ is Lord, to the glory of God the Father." He's given us His name to use it for our requests.

Satan is a name. The name of Jesus is far above that name. The spirits of crime, disease, drugs, lack, poverty, etc., are trying to come in and take control of areas around you. You have the authority to resist and bind all of these spirits or names in the name of Jesus.

Cancer is a name, poverty is a name, and recession is a name. Arthritis, heart trouble, etc.—all are names. We must recognize that each one of these names has to bow its knee and be subject to the name of Jesus.

You're not to be controlled by the thoughts of the world. There should be no place in your life for depression, discouragement, oppression, or self-doubt. This is possible if your mind is based on the thoughts that come from the Holy Spirit. Every time you think thoughts contrary to the Word of God, take control of them in the name of Jesus. Every conflicting thought has to bow its knee to the name of Jesus.

The angels respond to the name of Jesus.

The angels respond to the name of Jesus. When you quote Scripture to overcome the problem you have, you can loose the angelic forces to take care of that problem in the name of Jesus. They then have to obey the words of God that you are quoting. These will bring answers to your problems.

When Jesus sent out the seventy whom He appointed to announce the Kingdom of God, He said to them "'And heal the sick, and say to them, "The kingdom of God has come near to you'"" (Luke 10:9). When they returned from their mission trip, they reported, "'Lord, even the demons are subject to us in Your name'" (v. 17). The coming of God's Kingdom and the ministry of healing are not separated. The Holy Spirit delights to confirm the presence of the Kingdom by glorifying the power of the King.

Whenever you are praying for the sick, always pray in the name of Jesus. "And I will do whatever you ask in my name, so that the Son may bring glory to the Father'" (John 14:13, NIV). The elders in James 5:14 were commanded to pray in the name of Jesus. There is power in the name of Jesus!

Lay Hands on the Sick & Anoint Them with Oil

Healing the sick is part of our commission as believers. When we study the Scriptures we find there are gifts of healing given by the Holy Spirit, and also there are times when the Holy Spirit releases a special anointing to heal the sick. However, at all times we're commissioned to lay hands on the sick in faith, knowing that God will heal. "'They will lay hands on the sick, and they will recover,'" Jesus said (Mark 16:18). Again this commission is to all believers.

The first method that Jesus endorsed to heal the sick in the Great Commission was that of laying on of hands. Many times Jesus Himself used this method. The practice of "laying on of hands" is one of the foundational doctrines of the Christian faith as recorded in Hebrews 6:1-2—"Therefore, leaving the discussion of the elementary *principles* of Christ, let us go on to perfection, not laying again the foundation of repentance from dead works and of faith toward God, of the doctrine of baptisms, of laying on of hands, of resurrection of the dead, and of eternal judgment."

Right from the book of Genesis and on throughout God's Word, we see many examples of the principle of laying on of hands. Let's look as some examples and then see the power of laying on of hands for healing of physical bodies.

In the Old Testament, the laying on of hands often conferred *spiritual blessings.* Israel stretched out his hands on the two sons of Joseph as a blessing (Genesis 48:12-14). When Israel placed his right hand on the head of Ephraim, he imparted the blessing of the first born upon the last born. In other words, Manasseh, who was the oldest, didn't receive his firstborn blessing. It went to his younger brother Ephraim. Still, Manasseh was blessed. Speaking words of wisdom, Israel's hands were prophetically guided by the Holy Ghost in the blessing.

Jesus often laid hands on children and blessed them. My father consistently practices this principle. Often at night, he came into our rooms and laid his hands on us, prayed, and blessed us by speaking the promises of God's Word over our lives. All through my school days, before we walked out of our house, my mom and dad would lay hands on us three brothers and speak the promises of God's Word in pronouncement of blessings for the day. If you are a parent, I would encourage you to daily lay hands on your children and impart the blessing that God's Word promises.

> **If you are a parent, I would encourage you to daily lay hands on your children and impart the blessing that God's Word promises.**

Another practice of laying on of hands in Scripture is for the purpose of *setting aside leaders like deacons and elders for the work of the ministry and also sending ambassadors from the local church into mission fields.* When Moses was soon to die, "The Lord said to Moses: 'Take Joshua the son of Nun with you, a man in whom *is* the Spirit, and lay your hand on him; set him before Eleazar the priest and before all the congregation, and inaugurate him in their sight'" (Numbers 27:18-19). Because the Lord had commanded Moses to do this, the children of Israel listened to Joshua as their divinely-appointed leader.

At the church in Antioch, the Holy Ghost separated Paul and Barnabas for the work, and the prophets and teachers laid hands upon them and sent them on their way in the power of the Holy Ghost (Acts 13:1-3). Today, officers of the church have hands laid on them by those who confer the authority of the Holy Ghost to equip those who will serve in the church. The officers of the early church were ordained by prayer, fasting, and the laying on of hands. This action did not equip them with spiritual gifts. The seven deacons of Acts were men chosen already "full of the Holy Spirit and wisdom" (Acts 6:3). The ordination didn't qualify them. True servants of God are ordained because they are qualified, not qualified by being ordained.

True servants of God are ordained because they are qualified, not qualified by being ordained.

The laying on of hands can also serve as a means of *impartation of authority and the anointing of the Holy Spirit for a specific task*. When Elisha fell sick and was about to die, Joash, the king of Israel, came and wept over him. Elisha told the king to take a bow and arrow and put his hand upon the bow and Elisha put his hands over the king's hands. Elisha instructed the king to open the east window and shoot the arrow as "the arrow of the Lord's deliverance" (2 Kings 13:17). Furthermore, Elisha told the king, "For you must strike the Syrians at Aphek till you have destroyed them" (v. 17). Elisha laying his hands on the king's hands represented the divine impartation through Elisha to the king as the appointed leader who would deliver Israel. The shooting of the arrow represented the defeat. This acknowledged both an impartation of leadership and the special grace and anointing to accomplish God's will.

Paul reminded Timothy to stir up the fire of God or the anointing of the Holy Spirit in his life. "That is why I would remind you to stir up (rekindle the embers of, fan the flame of, and keep burning) the [gracious] gift of God, [the inner fire] that is in you by means of the laying on of my hands [with those of the elders at your ordination]" (2 Timothy 1:6, AMP).

The laying on of hands may be used for the purpose of *imparting spiritual gifts in relation to your calling*. Timothy had received spiritual gifts and anointing in his life through prophecies spoken over him as the elders laid hands on him—"Do not neglect the gift that is in you, which was given to you by prophecy with the laying on of the hands of the eldership" (1 Timothy 4:14).

The apostle Paul visited churches to pray for leaders and to impart spiritual gifts. He wrote the Roman believers, "For I long to see you, that I may impart to you some spiritual gift, so that you may be established" (1:11). People often make the mistake of reading this verse and wondering how one man can pray and impart gifts to so many people. Others say things like, "You can't impart what you don't have."

What people fail to see in impartation is that impartation isn't only taking what's in your life and imparting it to others, but it also involves simply serving as a conduit for God to impart something from Himself. We need to understand the impartation of spiritual gifts always is in relation to a person's calling. You can't lay hands on people and impart things that aren't ordained of God for that person's life.

> You can't lay hands on people and impart things that aren't ordained of God for that person's life.

Additionally, the laying of hands was used in Scripture *to help others receive the baptism in the Holy Spirit.* Many today have received the baptism in the Holy Spirit by the laying on of hands. This isn't the only way to receive the baptism but is one of the ways. At Pentecost, the Holy Ghost was given to the whole group through the spontaneous action of God.

The Holy Ghost came upon those at Ephesus that Paul would lay hands on and they spoke in tongues and prophesied (Acts 19:6). Peter and John laid hands upon the Samaritans, and they received the Holy Ghost (Acts 8:17). The reality of the Holy Ghost had to be readily apparent for Simon the sorcerer because he offered money to the apostles for the power of laying on of hands. Simon believed, but his heart wasn't right. Peter rebuked Simon saying, "'Your money perish with you, because you have thought that the gift of God may be purchased with money!'" (Acts 8:20).

We also see the laying on of hands used *for dedication and consecration.* The best example of this is when Simeon dedicated Jesus.

And behold, there was a man in Jerusalem whose name *was* Simeon, and this man *was* just and devout, waiting for the Consolation of Israel, and the Holy Spirit was upon him. And it had been revealed to him by the Holy Spirit that he would not see death before he had seen the Lord's Christ. So he came by the Spirit into the temple. And when the parents brought in the Child Jesus, to do for Him according to the custom of the law, he took Him up in his arms and blessed God and said: "Lord, now You are letting Your servant depart in peace, According to Your word; for my eyes have seen Your salvation . . ." (Luke 2:25-30).

One of the most common uses of the laying on of hands in Scripture is *for ministering healing and deliverance.* The New Testament is full of examples of Jesus and the apostles ministering healing and deliverance by the laying on of hands. The laying on of hands is an act of faith in cooperation with the Holy Ghost and obedience to the Word. A leprous man was considered to be unclean; Jesus stretched forth His hand in love and touched the leper, and he was made whole. Jesus touched people with blind eyes, and they saw. He touched ears, and they were opened. He touched the tongue of someone, and he began to speak. He touched the hand of Peter's mother-in-law, and fever left her. Jesus took the daughter of Jairus by the hand, and she arose from the dead. A woman had a bowed back for eighteen years, and Jesus laid His hands on her, and she was immediately made straight. In His own town of Nazareth because of their unbelief, Jesus could do no mighty works but He did lay His hands on a few sick and healed them (Mark 6:1-4).

The book of Acts is full of examples of the apostles using their hands with the same power that Jesus had, having "many signs and wonders" (2:43). Ananias laid his hands on Paul, restoring his sight. Paul healed many by the laying on of hands, and God's power is described as "special miracles by the hands of Paul" (Acts 19:11). When Paul laid his hands on the father of Publius and healed him, others also came and were healed—so many that they were honored with an abundance of necessary provisions.

Before Jesus was received into heaven, He told us that those that believe in the gospel and are baptized will also be able to lay hands on the sick in His name, and they will recover. According to this, any believer can lay hands upon the sick and expect them to be healed. You want the power to heal? Remember this promise from Jesus. Being in His name is being a part of His body and in fellowship with all who know Him. Our authority is delegated authority and not from our own personal power or goodness. We must believe in an all-powerful, loving limitless God, One who can accomplish these things.

> God is the Source of power; your hands are simply channels to bring the power to the sick person.

Your hands are anointed to transmit power, so that the body can recover because God is backing up the principle as you obey Him. No magic is in the hands. Obedience and faith bring healing to a person. It's not you; it's God. God is the Source of power; your hands are simply channels to bring the power to the sick person.

I've heard people claim they have healing properties in their hands; sometimes even believers claim this. Typically, psychic healers, spiritualists, and those involved in the occult claim to have healing powers in their hands. There are no healing properties in any human hands, but everyone's hands can be channels to release the power of God if we have faith in God to heal the sick. We believers need to understand that it's God working in us, through His Holy Spirit, and that's what brings healing to a sick person. God is always the Source of healing.

Whenever I've taught the doctrine of laying on of hands, I've been asked two questions based on Scripture. The first is—"What about Paul's saying to Timothy, 'Do not lay hands on anyone hastily, nor share in other people's sins; keep yourself pure'?" (1 Timothy 5:22). "If I allow people to lay hands on me," some have reasoned, "I might get a wrong spirit or curse on my life."

In my church, almost every Sunday, I encourage our people to go and lay hands on one another and pray for each other for healing and other needs. There are those who are concerned that some demon could jump on them or something, so they're not sure about letting another person lay hands on them. This practice in our church is watched over so that no outsider (non-member) does anything crazy or inappropriate. We've seen many people who have come in for the first time, who have been prayed for with the laying on of hands by some members in our church, and these guests have received healing. This has encouraged our members, helping them see how they can be used of the Lord to bring blessing to another.

Of course, as with other things, whenever something genuine is happening, the Devil will try to do something to stop the principles of the Word of God. We've had many people come to church who weren't members, and these have attempted to lay hands on people, speaking negative things to them. We stopped such people. When ministering to people, our job is to minister life. Anything that doesn't minister life isn't the pattern of Jesus. So I think when someone is ministering to you, and it's not life, you can stop that person. You should never be afraid that a wrong spirit will come upon you. You have the Holy Spirit in you. The Bible says, "'He who is in you is greater than he who is in the world'" (1 John 4:4).

When ministering to people, our job is to minister life. Anything that does not minister life isn't the pattern of Jesus.

Going back to the verse in 1 Timothy, when Paul wrote that verse, we need to read it in the context of the theme being addressed. Paul was addressing the leaders and telling them not to suddenly lay hands on people and set them aside for leadership without first knowing them and knowing if they were qualified or not. It isn't talking about praying for healing and ministering life to the needs of people. In many churches the pastors and those in leadership feel pressured to ordain someone out of status, influence, or the amount of money they give every month. I've known churches where a known personality or a president of a huge company was ordained as a leader within a few months after his born-again experience. Just because someone can manage a huge company doesn't mean he can manage God's house. The building of God's house isn't something to be taken lightly, and it can't be done with human wisdom alone. We must not lay hands on someone that God isn't ready to put His hand on.

The second question that I'm usually asked regarding laying on of hands has to do with anointing with oil. More specifically, I'm asked, "Is laying on of hand the same thing as anointing with oil?"

James 5:14-15 endorses the methods of anointing with oil along with laying on of hands. I believe both acts are effective. In the laying on of hands, there is no mention that prayer is to be made, but the anointing of oil must be accompanied with prayer. Both of these acts are independent of each other and also can be combined together. We can't say that laying on of hands is more powerful than anointing with oil and prayer. Both are powerful. We use either method per the occasion. The epistle of James is addressed primarily to believers—the church. I believe the place where anointing of oil is to be practiced most is among believers. Although we can anoint with oil those that are unbelievers for we see the disciples of Jesus "cast out many demons, and anointed with oil many who were sick, and healed *them*" (Mark 6:13).

> **Laying on of hands and the anointing of oil are simply channels. They are the taps that release the water, so to speak.**

The healing isn't in the oil, just as the healing isn't in the hands laid on a person's head. The healer is God, and the healing is manifested in response to faith. Laying on of hands and the anointing of oil are simply channels. They are the taps that release the water, so to speak. The anointing of oil needs to be accompanied with the prayer of faith. Every pastor and elder needs to practice the power of laying on of hands, anointing with oil, and invoking the name of Jesus with faith to see the power of God manifest in sick bodies.

Healing through Deliverance

Deliverance is a word that makes a lot of people feel uncomfortable, yet it is a word used throughout the Bible. The idea of deliverance is to set people free from any evil bondage. In the Old Testament, the words *deliverance* and *deliver* were used to set people free from evil rulers who were a type of Satan. For example, Pharaoh was a type of Satan who ruled over the Israelites in Egypt and was a cruel leader. He was against God and His laws, so God delivered them from bondage through his servant Moses.

Later on, the King of Babylon, also a type of Satan, tormented the people of God, so God said to them, "'Do not be afraid of the king of Babylon, of whom you are afraid; do not be afraid of him,' says the Lord, 'for I *am* with you, to save you and deliver you from his hand'" (Jeremiah 42:11). Throughout the Old Testament, the idea of deliverance was to set people free from bondage as a people and a nation who had been made slaves.

In the New Testament, the idea of deliverance is given a new picture. Deliverance in the New Testament was commonly spoken about individuals who were oppressed by the powers of Satan, or people who had allowed certain parts of their lives to be controlled by the enemy, but were freed by the Holy Spirit of God.

> The greatest demonstration of deliverance is when a person becomes a child in the Kingdom of God.

The greatest demonstration of deliverance is when a person becomes a child in the Kingdom of God. That person is delivered from the dominion of sin and Satan.

In regards to receiving healing through deliverance, the four gospels record nineteen different accounts of specific healings under the ministry of Jesus. Of the nineteen, there were eleven whose problems were caused by a demon spirit. Keep in mind that there is only one Devil but many demons.

When we study the ministry of Jesus, we find that Jesus, on a regular basis, dealt with demons. Although the Old Testament notes the presence and activity of demons on many occasions, we never find any ministry of a person expelling demons until Jesus. The Scriptures disclose some people who tried to expel demons but not by the authority of Jesus. Their attempts were through some evil practices.

The expelling of demons was the most striking feature of the ministry of Jesus compared to any other person used of God before His time. There are historical records of the resurrection of the dead, of miracles, of healing, and of multiplication of food, but only the New Testament has records of the expelling of demons.

It's most amazing to observe the ministry of deliverance in the life of Jesus. Most of the time, we would think He was expelling demons from people who were not believers. Most of the people Jesus delivered, however, were religious Jews. These were believers of the Law and of the traditional history passed down from their forefathers. I've seen people who are born again, filled with the Holy Spirit and speaking in tongues in need of deliverance because they've opened a certain area of their lives to the control of the Devil. I've also seen many who wouldn't take personal responsibility for their sin and just blamed everything on the Devil. So I must make it clear that many have allowed the Devil to gain a foothold in their lives by allowing bitterness, unforgiveness, hatred, etc.

As we look to the Scriptures in regards to the work of Satan through demons, remember that Jesus never commissioned anyone in the Scriptures to go and preach the gospel without commissioning them to cast out (expel) demons—"And these signs will follow those who believe: In My name they will cast out demons; they will speak with new tongues" (Mark 16:17).

The real you is your spirit, not your body.

Demons are evil spirits who have no body of their own, so they seek expression through other forms of physical bodies of man or of animals. This is similar to us; we're spirit beings, we have minds, and we live in physical bodies. The real you is your spirit, not your body. Your body helps you give expression to your spirit. You can taste, feel, smell, hear, and see thanks to your body. In the same manner, demons want a body to express their evil nature, so they are looking for that opportunity.

I firmly believe that anything to do with the Kingdom of God is always pictured by light and anything to do with the Kingdom of the Satan is pictured by darkness. Wherever there is darkness, Satan and his demons are free to roam around. It says in Luke 11:35, "'Therefore take heed that the light which is in you is not darkness.'" It simply means that we shouldn't allow anything of darkness in our lives; otherwise, Satan and his demons have permission to roam in that area.

When people open up parts of their lives to darkness, demons use those areas to inflict sickness. A person can have one demon or several at once. On one occasion, a demon admitted to Jesus that his name was Legion, "for we are many'" (Mark 5:9; Luke 8:30). We find several occasions in the Scripture where Jesus expelled numerous demons at one time from a single person (Luke 8:30).

While expelling demons, I've observed they will try to make the situation comical and not serious. They do this by making funny faces, funny sounds, and poking fun at the elements of Christian belief. I've heard and seen people who need deliverance, sing songs and dance to non-Christian songs and call Satan king, ruler, leader, guru, hero, etc. Always control the situation by speaking the Word of God and the name of Jesus to maintain order.

Several instances in the Scripture show that people were healed as the evil spirits or demons were expelled.

Several instances in the Scripture show that people were healed as the evil spirits or demons were expelled. In Luke 13:11, the woman who had been plagued for 18 years with the spirit of infirmity was bent over and could not straighten herself up. Jesus told her, "'Woman, you are loosed from your infirmity'" (Luke 13:12). He laid His hands on her, "and immediately she was made straight" (Luke 13:13).

When I started preaching the gospel, I began to see a lot of people that were healed come back few months later for healing of another type of sickness. Some people got healed three or four times of different sicknesses, each after another. I wondered why, and then I realized a sickness may be controlled by a spirit. You have to rebuke and cast out the spirit, and then the sickness will go. If the person is healed and the spirit isn't cast out, it will manifest in other sicknesses. As believers, we have to learn not only to receive our miracle and healing but to maintain it, enlarge it, and multiply it.

We need to allow the Holy Spirit to speak and direct us in how we should go about ministering to the person.

There are several things to keep in mind when ministering deliverance. Listen to the voice of the Holy Spirit. We need to allow the Holy Spirit to speak and direct us in how we should go about ministering to the person. He can tell us the root of the problem. I've discovered that people don't get healed because their root problem is unforgiveness or some sinful habit which the person doesn't want to let go of. So when we listen to the Holy Spirit, we can minister and bring healing to that person.

Once a man came who had several sicknesses in his body. He had a whole list of them. As we prayed for him, he started to manifest demons, vomit, and display anger. We knew this was not him but the demons. We commanded the demons to leave, and he was set free but still wasn't healed because he had some root issues. He was molested when he was a child and had an abusive father. Due to this torment, he always was involved in heavy pornography. Once he was set free from demons, we prayed with him, the Holy Spirit began to reveal things about his life, and we walked him through the process of renouncing sins in his life, forgiving his father, and the person who molested him. Once he found freedom, we simply released healing to his body, and he was made whole.

Secondly, don't fear Satan and his demons. Many are afraid of Satan and his demons. Some are so afraid that they say, "Don't say anything about Satan, or something bad will happen." As a believer, we should not be afraid of Satan and his demons. We're free from his control over our lives. The Bible says in 1 John 4:4, "You are of God, little children, and have overcome them, because He who is in you is greater than he who is in the world."

God has given you power over the Devil and his demons. They are subject to you in the name of Jesus. Jesus said, "'Behold, I give you the authority to trample on serpents and scorpions, and over all the power of the enemy, and nothing shall by any means hurt you. Nevertheless do not rejoice in this, that the spirits are subject to you, but rather rejoice because your names are written in heaven'" (Luke 10:19-20).

Thirdly, command the demon(s) to come out and declare the person free. I was in a crusade where many were getting born again and others were coming to be prayed for. We had prayer teams go and pray for the people. As I was overseeing teams who were praying for people, I noticed there were lots of people manifesting demons. One particular incidence I saw really angered me. A person was manifesting, and there was a group of believers holding hands together and just praying in tongues. This isn't the way to minister deliverance and healing. When we pray in tongues, we speak to God. What needs to be done in this situation is the demon needs to be addressed and commanded to leave the person. We're not praying for the person; we're commanding the demons to leave. Once that person is free, we can begin praying for the person and start speaking blessing.

There is no evidence in the Scriptures that we need to find out the name first, or have lengthy conversations with demons.

I've seen those who don't know how to bring deliverance to people. It's good to speak in tongues, but while you're doing that the demons are at the center of attentions and are causing a commotion. You have authority in Jesus' name. Use it and free the person.

Remember you are addressing the demons first and then praying for the person later. There is no evidence in the Scriptures that we need to find out the name first, or have lengthy conversations with demons. Often, you will know by the Spirit of God what type of spirit is controlling that person. You call that spirit by name and command it to leave. With the demonized mute boy, Jesus said, "'Deaf and dumb spirit, I command you, come out of him and enter him no more!' Then *the spirit* cried out, convulsed him greatly, and came out of him. And he became as one dead, so that many said, 'He is dead.' But Jesus took him by the hand and lifted him up, and he arose" (Mark 9:25–27). I don't encourage people to ask the demons their names because they will lie anyway. The point is freeing the person from any control of the Devil and his demons.

Lastly, start building a prayer hedge around that person and teaching him how to build a prayer hedge around himself. Once a person is free, the Bible says that an evil spirit returns if the house is empty.

> "When an unclean spirit goes out of a man, he goes through dry places, seeking rest, and finds none. Then he says, 'I will return to my house from which I came.' And when he comes, he finds *it* empty, swept, and put in order. Then he goes and takes with him seven other spirits more wicked than himself, and they enter and dwell there; and the last *state* of that man is worse than the first. So shall it also be with this wicked generation" (Matthew 12:43-45).

Begin to fill the person's life with the Word of God, and if she is ignorant of how to do it herself, then work with her. All the areas that she has been freed from need to be refilled with the principle of the Kingdom of God, and then she must consistently build a prayer hedge around her healing. The Bible says in Ecclesiastes 10:8 that "he who digs a pit [for others] will fall into it, and whoever breaks through a fence *or* a [stone] wall, a serpent will bite him" (AMP).

Remember, you are a channel to release life to people. Begin walking in faith, believing that God is able and willing to heal all sickness and disease. May you be used to cause others to proclaim, "Christ is my Healer!"

References

Bits & Pieces (June 24, 1993) 3.

Booth, William. "The Founder's Message to Soldiers,"
Christianity Today (October 5, 1992) 48.

Hewitt, James S. *Finding God's Resources*
(Wheaton: Tyndale House Publishers, 1988) 242.

Oyakhilome, Rev. Chris. *None of These Diseases* (Lawrenceville,
Georgia: To His Glory Publishing, 2005) 48.

Strong, James. *Strong's Exhaustive Concordance of the Bible*
(Nashville: Abingdon Press, 1986).

10,000 Sermon Illustrations Software (Garland, Texas:
Biblical Studies Press, LLC–Galaxie Software).

Wiersbe, Warren. *The Bible Exposition Commentary:
New Testament: Volume 1* (Colorado Springs: Victor, 2001) 180.

Wiersbe, Warren. *The Integrity Crisis*
(Nashville: Thomas Nelson Publishers, 1991) 119.

For more information about Pastor Nicky S. Raiborde
or for other audio and videos resources,
please contact:

Fresh Focus Media,
A division of International Family Church
1311 Marley Drive
Columbia, SC 29210
Phone: 803.731.0089
E-mail: ifcsc@hotmail.com
Web site: www.daniel1132.com

CPSIA information can be obtained at www.ICGtesting.com
Printed in the USA
LVOW12s2327260216

476899LV00001B/2/P

9 780980 019643